# THE
# MAN
## WHO GREW
## TWO BREASTS

*and Other True Tales
of Medical Detection*

BERTON ROUECHÉ

# THE MAN

## WHO GREW
## TWO BREASTS

*and Other True Tales
of Medical Detection*

MJF BOOKS
NEW YORK

Published by MJF Books
Fine Communications
322 Eighth Avenue
New York, NY 10001

*The Man Who Grew Two Breasts*
LC Control Number: 2009932339
ISBN-13: 978-1-56731-973-6
ISBN-10: 1-56731-973-4

# Contents

# THE
# MAN
## WHO GREW
## TWO BREASTS

*and Other True Tales
of Medical Detection*

# The Man Who Grew
# Two Breasts

One midwinter morning in 1979, a seventy-year-old man whom I'll call Harry Lee Patterson, the owner of a lumberyard in Franklin, Tennessee (population 31,983), was drying himself after a shower when his fingers brushed against what felt like a lump on his left breast. He dropped the towel and looked at himself in the bathroom mirror. Patterson had been half aware for several weeks of a swelling there but had taken it to be, like his expanding waistline, simply one of the changes of age. But this morning it had a different look. It was no mere swelling. It was now a lump, and a lump in the shape of a tiny, female breast—areoled, nippled, and even a little sensitive to the touch. It was (as he described it to himself) about the size of a pecan. He was not an excitable man, but the sight of it gave him a breathless, sinking feeling. He hurried into his clothes and went downstairs and told his wife about it. He opened his shirt and showed it to her. She was as disconcerted as he. The idea of a man, an elderly man, developing a womanly breast, however small, was almost beyond belief. It was also, of course, alarming.

Patterson went to the telephone and called his doctor, the family doctor. The doctor heard him out without comment, and gave him an early afternoon appointment. Patterson was more than punctual, but the doctor saw him at once. He knew Patterson to be in good health for his age, and he examined the little breast with care and concern. He saw there something that he had never seen before, but he recognized it almost immediately as a case of gynecomastia. Gynecomastia, as breast enlargement in a male is known to medicine, is not a common occurrence, but it is far from rare. Its immediate cause is an excess in the blood of the female hormone estrogen. Gynecomastia is a frequent phenomenon in puberty, and a frequent source of embarrassment, but, with few exceptions, it soon resolves itself. The estrogen is overwhelmed at a certain stage by a surge of testosterone, the male hormone, that marks the premiere of sexual maturity. In a young boy, however, or in a man of fifty or more, gynecomastia can be, and often is, a serious affliction. The estrogen that excites the male breast to a feminine enhancement can come from various sources—drugs, liver disease, cancer. The enlargement of a single breast is uncomfortably suggestive of an emerging tumor, and one most commonly situated in the affected breast. Bilateral gynecomastia, the simultaneous enlargement of both breasts, has a much more favorable prognosis. Its sources of estrogen are generally located elsewhere.

The doctor explained all this to Patterson. It was his understanding, he said, that the prudent treatment of a unilateral gynecomastia was a total mastectomy. A pathological examination of the excised tissue could then determine the presence or absence of malignancy. There was no other way to resolve the question. And the procedure should be done as quickly as possible. The physiology of the male breast is much less complicated than that of the female breast, and this enables a malignant tumor to rapidly metastasize. On the other hand, this simpler physiology requires a less invasive surgery. He proposed that he refer Patterson to a surgeon of his acquaintance at the Vanderbilt University School of Medicine, in Nashville. Patterson said he was willing, as always, to take the doctor's advice.

The doctor made the necessary arrangements, and a day or two later Patterson and his wife, reassuring each other with the doctor's reassurances, drove up to Nashville, some twenty miles to the north, and met the recommended surgeon. The surgeon agreed with both his colleague's diagnosis and his sense of urgency, and arranged for Patterson to undergo the usual preoperative examinations. He confirmed that the procedure was not severely invasive. It could, and would, be done on an outpatient basis. The surgery was performed the next day but one, and the incision was quickly and cleanly closed. Patterson would be left with no more than a hairline scar. The excised tissue was sent to the pathological laboratory. The pathologist's report came through the following day. There was no sign of a malignancy, or even a tumor. The conclusion read: "Benign gynecomastia." The Pattersons drove back to Franklin under the natural impression that the strange and frightening episode was over, that all was well again.

That was around the end of February. The weeks went by and Patterson's incision healed as promised. His gynecomastic experience faded from his mind. Then, one day in early May, the memory was abruptly revived. He noticed—there was no mistaking it—that his *right* breast was a little enlarged, beginning to take on a familiar feminine look. Patterson reacted much as before. This time, however, he was more bewildered than alarmed. There had been no mention by either his doctor or by the surgeon of a possible recurrence. But there it was. He called and talked with his doctor. The doctor, as before, attempted to reassure him, and referred him again to the Vanderbilt surgeon. The surgeon reconsidered the case. Its belated bilaterality removed this gynecomastia from the surgical to the medical field. The pressing necessity now was to determine the source of the feminizing hormone. That was a matter for a specialist, an endocrinologist. He said he had a colleague, a professor of medicine here at Vanderbilt, in mind. He was an endocrinologist of experience and distinction. His name was Clifton K. Meador. The surgeon said he would speak to Dr. Meador and arrange for a consultation.

I went down to Nashville not long ago and talked with Dr. Meador about his role in the Patterson case. I was late by a dozen years or more, but it was a case, a diagnostic dilemma, that he is unlikely to ever forget. While retaining his professorship at Vanderbilt, Dr. Meador is now director of medicine at St. Thomas Hospital, a Vanderbilt teaching affiliate, and he received me in his office there. He is a tall, immaculate man in his sixties, with china blue eyes and a senatorial turbulence of thick white hair. He was born and raised in Selma, Alabama (before it became famous), and is a graduate of Vanderbilt University and of the Vanderbilt School of Medicine. He served his internship in New York, at Columbia Presbyterian Hospital, his only considerable sojourn in the North, before circling back to Nashville and Vanderbilt. His office, like most of its kind, was a functional clutter of bookcases and filing cabinets, with a desk, two chairs, and a coatrack. On a wall near the coatrack hung a large, framed notice. It was headed: Fee Bill. Physicians of Selma, Alabama. April, 1893. Below that was a list of categories. I noted down some of them. Day visit & Rx: $2.00. A night visit was $4.00. Labor, maternal care & services, 5 days: $15 to $25.

"A souvenir," Dr. Meador told me. "Those visits, of course, were house calls." He turned over some papers on his desk. "Well, I saw Harry Lee Patterson for the first time around the middle of May. He impressed me. He was into his seventies and looked no more than fifty. He looked to be in good health. He was thin—maybe lean is a better word. After we had talked for a few minutes, he seemed relaxed and comfortable with me. I'd seen his chart and talked with the other doctors. I had no reservations about the treatment he had received. Mastectomy was clearly indicated. There was no other way of determining if his gynecomastia was malignant. He stripped and I looked him over very thoroughly. His right breast was quite conspicuously enlarged. I remember it as about three centimeters in size—a good inch and a half. I was not too confounded by the unilaterality. I had seen it before. There is sometimes a lag in the response of the breasts to what is most certainly a common estrogen source. I don't know why. But I know that it happens. What did concern me was the appearance of gynecomastia in a man of Patterson's age. That usually means the presence of a malignant tumor of the testicles or of the adrenal glands. In an adult male those are the only endogenous sources of the female hormone. Both of these normally secrete very small amounts of estrogen. These secretions are essentially harmless. But a tumor in either of those areas can produce enormous amounts, and such tumors are highly malignant. They grow very fast and spread—metastasize—very rapidly. There is a very narrow window of time when surgical removal can be curative. I didn't have any time to waste.

"It is sometimes possible to detect a testicular tumor or a tumor of the adrenals by physical examination—by feel. I palpated his testicles, feeling for masses. Everything felt normal. The adrenals are located just above the kidneys. I pushed here and there, trying to feel his deep-seated adrenals. If there was anything there, I couldn't find it. So much for that approach. But I just wasn't satisfied. I mean, I couldn't believe it. So I went back and tried all over again. Everything still felt normal. Well, that was only the usual beginning. There were other approaches. One of these was an examination in several ways of his urine. One involved mice, another was a chemical search for estrogen, and a third measured the testosterone level. I sent Patterson home with instructions to collect all of his urine for twenty-four hours. Which he did. Then I asked for another twenty-four-hour collection. And then a third. Each of the tests required a different specimen. I also drew a sample of blood. The tests would be done in a laboratory in California. I would have the results in about three weeks. That was a painful wait. But that was 1979. There have been great advances in laboratory technology since then. The tests I was waiting for can now be done in a day or two. The results came back on schedule. I was stunned. They all were normal. I couldn't believe it. Somebody must have screwed up. Or there was something wrong with those specimens. This is a subject I have strong feelings about. I am only too familiar with false negatives. False negatives are a diagnostic pitfall—especially in a case like this, when the trouble is serious. So I asked for a repeat—more specimens and another round of tests. Which meant another three-week wait.

"I have to say I was worried. I was far more worried than he was. He seemed to be happy to leave everything to me. He just wasn't fully aware of the possibilities. That window of time was narrowing. Meanwhile, I arranged for some X rays of his testicles and of his adrenals. And also a chest X ray. Lung cancer can sometimes stimulate the production of large quantities of estrogen. But that was another dead end. The readings all were normal. I waited for the test results from California—for one of those negatives to come back positive. Then I would know what to do. They finally came. Still negative. There was nothing to do but accept it. But one thing was certain. Something inside him was making some estrogen. He could be secreting some sort of hybrid estrogen. The secretion could be at a level those tests just couldn't see. I tried to think—what was I missing? I still had tumors on my mind. The next time he came in I went over him from head to toe, feeling everywhere for anything that felt like a mass. Any kind of cancer can conceivably make some hormone. There was nothing anywhere that I could feel. I ordered some CT scans—chest, abdomen, even his head. The pituitary gland is attached to the base of the brain, and a tumor there could be the source. I was on a fishing expedition, but I knew what I was doing. He simply had to have a tumor hiding out somewhere. Tumors can be very small—no bigger than a piece of pencil lead. I didn't want to miss any possible malignancy that might still be surgically removable. But the imaging told me nothing. I was really at a blind end, totally baffled. I talked to a colleague, a man I greatly admire, and he joined me in my next consultation with Patterson. His breast, I might say, was getting quite conspicuous by now. My friend couldn't suggest anything that I hadn't done. I was getting a little desperate. The next time Patterson came in I got up the nerve to ask him if he smoked marijuana. A lot of heavy pot smokers develop gynecomastia. He didn't seem the type. But. He gave me a look. He said, 'What do you think I am—one of those long-haired dope fiends?' "

Dr. Meador smiled at the memory and shook his head. "But you know," he said, "that marijuana impulse did something for me. It turned my attention away from cancer. And somehow I happened to remember a case I had seen quite a few years before. The patient was a little boy about six years old. He had developed gynecomastia at the age of five. Gynecomastia at that age is every bit as ominous as it is in a man of seventy. The list of possible sources is as full of cancers, maybe more so. I worked him up as carefully as I did Patterson. And I was completely baffled. I remember asking his mother if he might be getting into her birth control pills or some other compound that might contain estrogen. The answer was no. She didn't use the pill or anything on that order. She volunteered that the boy did take some vitamins on a regular, daily basis. That didn't seem to lead anywhere. But all of a sudden, it did. I was looking something up in the journal *Pediatrics* and I came across a report on vitamins being contaminated during manufacture. A single stamping machine was used to punch out vitamin tablets and estrogen pills. The paper named the brand name. I called the boy's mother—and sure enough. That was the brand he took. All I had to do was switch him to another brand and in a couple of months he was normal. But imagine! I mean, think of the minute amount of estrogen that the stamping machine passed on to the vitamin tablets. And what a profound physical effect it had. Remembering that case, I remembered another. It was a case I'd read about somewhere, an infant suffering from pseudoprecocious puberty. The source turned out to be a skin cream, an ointment containing estrogens.

"I brought up the subject of drugs, medications, with Patterson. I asked him to bring me everything he had in his medicine cabinet. I spelled it out—antibiotics, cold pills, decongestants, codeine, aspirin, laxatives, antacids, sleeping pills. He brought me what he had. He wasn't much of a pill taker. And it wasn't any help. I couldn't find anything that might connect. In certain cases, in cases like this, I like to have the patient keep a diary. A detailed daily record of their doings can sometimes turn up a clue. That, too, came to nothing. He simply refused. It was too much trouble. He had a business to run. He knew he might be in serious trouble, but that didn't seem to bother him much. I was taking care of him. Still, the diary idea had got him in a searching mood. I got him to thinking about what he was eating and drinking and breathing—everything he was taking into his system. Was he doing something he shouldn't be doing? Or not doing something he should? He did his best. He was very cooperative about that. But nothing he could think of helped. This was July. There couldn't be much time left. I retraced my steps. I got tumors on my mind again. I put him through all of the X-ray studies again. I couldn't help thinking that sooner or later he was going to show me a tumor. But, no. All of the studies, all of the repeats, gave the same results as before. I don't have to tell you how I felt. Here was an obvious and ominous abnormality, and I couldn't come up with a diagnosis."

Dr. Meador sat back in his chair. He gave me a curious look. "I didn't see Patterson for over a month," he said. "He and I had agreed to just go along and see what happened. There didn't seem to be anything else to do. Then one day he walked into my office with his wife. She was short and a little plump but quite attractive. She was about his age, with twice his personality. I'll call her Gladys. I knew her, but only slightly. They were both grinning, and Patterson blurted out: 'This was just too good to tell you over the phone. I want you to hear it for yourself. Gladys has made a diagnosis that you and I missed. Tell him, Gladys.'

"She told me. I can't remember just how she put it, but what she had to say was this. She and Patterson had always had a very active sex life. They still 'enjoyed' each other several times a week, almost as often as in their younger days. She told me all this with a big smile—not in the least embarrassed. But she had been troubled off and on for some years with an atrophic vaginitis. Atrophic vaginitis is an inflammation of the vagina. It occurs in postmenopausal women and is associated with an estrogen deficiency. Now she had my full attention. She said a vaginal cream had been prescribed for her trouble, and she had been using it as needed for the past eight years. But since around Christmas she had been using it much oftener—whenever they wanted to 'enjoy' themselves—simply as a lubricant. The other day, she said, something I had said to Harry Lee about what drugs he used got her to thinking. She took a good

11

look at the tube of vaginal cream, read some fine print on the back, and gathered that it contained estrogen. She had brought with her the instruction sheet that came in the package. She handed it over. The heading was Premarin (Conjugated Estrogens). I read on a bit, but that was enough. I looked up. She was watching me. She said: 'Tell me, Doctor. You don't suppose that has anything to do with Harry Lee's breasts, do you?' And she actually gave me a great big wink.

"That wasn't, of course, the end of the case. Although it really was. It was a very persuasive hypothesis, but it had to be tested and proved. It was also an astonishing idea. I had never heard of gynecomastia in men exposed to a vaginal cream. And later, when I checked the literature, there was nothing on record there. One thing I needed to know was the extent of the exposure. I determined that each gram of the cream contained 0.625 milligrams of conjugated estrogen. Gladys and I figured out that she was using about thirty-one grams of the cream a year, or almost two-thirds of a gram a day. How much estrogen Patterson absorbed each time they 'enjoyed' themselves could only be guessed. It was obviously enough to affect his breasts, but not enough to show up on any of these many tests. The proof I needed began to appear in about a month. Gladys had found a vaginal cream that contained no estrogen. And Patterson's breast began to shrink. By the end of the summer, it was back to normal. It was a wonderful diagnosis. It was brilliant. I only wish it had been mine."

# The Dinosaur
# Collection

**D**r. Vincent L. Guandolo, with whom I talked not long ago about the experience that has given his professional life an absorbing special interest, is a senior associate in a large and comprehensive pediatric group practice (five pediatricians and a pediatric ophthalmologist) in Gaithersburg, Maryland—an upper-middle-class dormitory suburb of Washington—and president-elect of the medical staff of Children's Hospital National Medical Center. It was, he told me, entirely by chance (or mischance) that it was he to whom the woman I'll call Laurie Starke—Mrs. Frank Starke—and her son, Kevin, were directed by the appointments nurse on the afternoon of March 16, 1977. He received them in one of the cheerful, nurserylike examination rooms. Mrs. Starke was a small, smiling, friendly woman in her late twenties, with long auburn hair and a beguiling southern accent. Kevin, whom she carried slung over her shoulder, was one month old.

"I can't say she was particularly attractive," Dr. Guandolo told me. We were sitting in the office library, a windowless, book-lined room with a conference table and chairs in the middle. There were books and papers on the table. "But maybe I'm a little prejudiced. I think of her as a combination of flower child and southern belle. Actually, I didn't form any real impressions at that first meeting. It was an ordinary well-baby visit. I took the family history. The Starkes had just moved to Gaithersburg—from Fayetteville, North Carolina. Kevin had been born in Fayetteville, which was Mrs. Starke's hometown. Her parents still lived there. Mr. Starke was a lawyer, and had just been hired as counsel by one of the federal agencies. They were very happy here. Kevin was normal in weight and development. Mrs. Starke had a question or two about nursing. She also thought he might have some nasal congestion. I was able to reassure her. That was it. I suggested another visit in about a month. Monthly visits are routine during a baby's first year." Dr. Guandolo picked up a kind of loose-leaf notebook. It was about the size of a Manhattan telephone directory, and almost as thick. "This is Kevin's chart," he said. "It's my record of his office visits. As you can see, each page is ruled for eleven visits. His first visit—the March sixteenth visit—is here at the top of page one. Date. Complaint. Comments. Treatment. Then comes the second visit. And so on." He riffled through the pages. "And on and on," he said. "There are two hundred and thirty-six of them."

Dr. Guandolo turned back to the first page of the chart. "The second visit was on Friday, April fifteenth, 1977," he said. "It was much like the first. No problems. So was the visit in May. And those in June, July, and August. Kevin was growing up very nicely. I thought Mrs. Starke seemed at times a little overly concerned about him, but that's not at all unusual in young and caring mothers. Toward the end of August, though, about a week after the regular monthly checkup, I got a telephone call from her. It was around ten o'clock in the morning. She sounded distraught. Kevin was sick. He had taken sick down in Fayetteville. They had driven there for the weekend. It was an ear infection. Also, he had an attack of bronchitis. She wanted me to see him at once, that afternoon. I rearranged my calendar, and told her to come in at one-fifteen. They arrived, as always, very punctually. They both looked very much as always. She was calm, unworried. Kevin looked just as he had the week before. I checked him over. His ears were normal, his chest was clear. I told Mrs. Starke that I could find nothing whatever the matter. She nodded her head, and agreed. She said he *was* much improved. She said it was probably because of the treatment he had received from a doctor down home. I asked her what treatment that was. It was an antibiotic, she said—an antibiotic called Keflex. That gave me something of a jolt. Keflex is cephalexin, a very powerful drug. It was hardly a drug that I would initially prescribe for a six-month-old baby. I had to wonder about that North Carolina doctor. Still, I had to admit, it certainly seemed to have done the job.

"I say it seemed to. Because Mrs. Starke called me again the very next week. She had to see me. She and her husband had been up most of the night with Kevin. He'd had a terrible coughing spell. He had trouble breathing. I said all right. I could only think it was some kind of relapse. She came in with him wrapped in a blanket. I looked him over very carefully. There was no sign of a cough. There was no nasal congestion. I found nothing. However, babies can go from sick to well in a very short time. I told her not to worry, and to call me if the trouble recurred. She left, as always, smiling.

"I think of that now as a point of beginning. I didn't see it at the time, of course, but something had changed, was changing. The visit after the weekend in Fayetteville, and the one the following week, seemed to have set a pattern. Instead of the normal routine of monthly visits, I found myself seeing Kevin every week. It was a scenario. Mrs. Starke would telephone me every week, usually on a Wednesday, for an emergency appointment. The complaints were always much the same. Nasal congestion. Or cough. Or ear pain. Or, once in a while, vomiting. And, always, my physical examination had the same negative results. No, there was one exception. In December, I think it was, I found a mild otitis media—a visible ear infection—and I prescribed an appropriate antibiotic. The frantic telephone calls and the uneventful visits continued into 1978. Kevin celebrated his first birthday. After the first birthday, it is usual to see a baby only every three months. But here I was seeing Kevin every week. It's hard to remember just how I felt at the time. I know I was getting a little tired of those weekly dramas. But I had no choice. A doctor can't ignore an emergency call—especially one involving an infant. There was one visit, on September twenty-second, 1978, that stands out in my memory. Mrs. Starke's call was unusually frantic. Kevin had had a fall. He had been riding in the carrier seat of her bicycle, and she had swerved to avoid a rock or something, and he had fallen out. I remember her saying, 'He didn't move for a long time.' There was no sign of a head injury, no bumps or swellings. He was alert. His eyes were normal. No neurological problems. I asked if he had vomited. She said no. Then there was another illness during a weekend in Fayetteville. It was a sudden, unexplained fever that spiked to one hundred five degrees. The Fayetteville doctor was called in, and he treated him with amoxicillin. Well, that was an improvement on Keflex. And, apparently, it cured him. I mean, I found him normal. A few weeks later—a few visits later—Mrs. Starke told me that Kevin had been wheezing. One of their neighbors was a doctor, she said—she called him Dr. Jack—and he came over and diagnosed croup. Well, almost everybody around here has a doctor neighbor. This is probably the most heavily doctored area in the country. Walter Reed is here, and the Naval Hospital, and the National Institutes of Health, and the Uniformed Services School of Medicine, and a whole lot more. Dr. Jack, I gathered from Mrs. Starke, was an oncologist.

Had he treated Kevin? Oh, yes—with Adrenalin. I thought to myself, You'd better stick to your tumors, Dr. Jack."

Dr. Guandolo stood up and stretched. "I get tired of sitting," he said. He walked around the table, turned, and walked back around the other way. He is a stocky man of around fifty, with dark, wavy hair and warm hazel eyes, and his walk is brisk. He sat down again. "I haven't said much about Mrs. Starke," he said. "She was an interesting woman. Different, anyway. I think of her as two people. She was one person on the telephone and another here in the office. On the telephone, she was more than an overly anxious mother; she was practically in hysterics. Here in the office, she was all sociability. She was always relaxed and cheerful. She was friendly with the whole office staff. She called them all by their first names, and they all called her Laurie. She told one of the nurses, ' "Mrs. Starke" is my mother-in-law.' I think she would have liked to be Laurie to me, too. She liked to bake, and she often brought us gifts of carrot cake or zucchini bread. Or homemade jellies. A few hours after a frantic emergency call, she would come bouncing in with Kevin over her shoulder and a loaf of bread in her hand. She would sometimes sit in one of the waiting rooms and talk baby problems with the other mothers while I was examining Kevin. When she came into the examination room, she would often sit down in a corner and bury herself in a book. It was usually a novel. She told me she had majored in English at the University of Virginia. Sometimes her book was a Russian history text. She was working on a graduate degree in

Russian history at Georgetown University. She often talked about herself and her family. She had two brothers. One of them, Paul, was a lawyer down in Fayetteville. The other, Patrick, was a doctor, a pediatric cardiologist on the staff of the Peter Bent Brigham Hospital, in Boston. He and his wife and their brain-damaged child were in England on some sort of sabbatical. Her father was a retired Presbyterian minister, and, I gathered, not well. She didn't often mention her husband. He seemed to travel a lot. I remember suggesting rather early on that I'd like to talk to him. She said, of course, but right now he was in Japan. Another time, he was on a three-month assignment in Vienna. I thought maybe that was it—that she was probably lonely. She never spoke of any friends. But she seemed to keep busy. She told me one day she was studying law. She was in her last year at Georgetown. She had a wonderful girl called Cindy who looked after Kevin when she was in class. I heard a lot about Cindy. Kevin was often taken sick when Cindy was with him. Cindy sometimes called Mrs. Starke at school. I think it was she who suggested to Mrs. Starke that Kevin might be suffering from some allergy. And, sure enough, an allergist friend of Dr. Jack had confirmed it. Kevin was in some sort of hyposensitization program. One afternoon, she came in with Kevin for one of the usual reasons, and she was wild with excitement. She had passed the bar. She was a lawyer, and she had been offered a job at the Georgetown Law Center. I congratulated her. But I remember thinking, What's going on here? What am I—her surrogate husband?"

Dr. Guandolo gave me a wry smile. "I didn't know

what to think," he said. "But Kevin was a good baby. I don't think I ever heard him cry. Still, there it was—it seemed he was always sick. It was usually an upper-respiratory-tract congestion or earache or vomiting. But I could never find anything wrong. I decided it might be good to have another, more specialized opinion. I asked an otolaryngologist to see him. Here's his report, in its entirety: 'Diagnosis: Normal ear, nose, and throat examination. Treatment: With the history of recurrent otitis media and normal ear examination today, I suggested adenoidectomy as an adjunct to allergy hyposensitization.' I didn't find that very helpful. It seemed a contradiction to recommend an operation on a normal throat. So I did nothing in that direction. I was more concerned about a new development. This was toward the end of 1978. Mrs. Starke's calls began to feature a new complaint. I have a note on a visit on December eighth. She called to tell me that Kevin had had a very bad night. He had vomited three times. He had also had what she called shaking spells. Several of them. My findings were negative. She brought him in again on December eleventh. He'd had another series of shaking spells. Along with much vomiting. He looked and acted perfectly normal to me. His weight was unchanged. His hydration was normal. Some dehydration would be expected after prolonged vomiting. I thought she must have exaggerated the vomiting. Vomiting in an infant can look worse than it is. A few days later, he had another bad shaking spell. With vomiting, as before. But what worried me a little was something new. She said that during one of the shaking spells his legs began to jerk. That sounded uncomfortably like some sort of seizure. I thought a thorough neurological examination was in order, and I made arrangements with a pediatric-neurologist colleague. I got his report on December twenty-ninth. It covered three typewritten pages. Here is his conclusion: 'This toddler seems entirely normal. The story is not a strong one for increased intracranial pressure being responsible for the vomiting. I have no good idea as to what this spell was last week, but seriously doubt that it was any epileptic seizure. I would certainly not want to treat him as such at this point unless his EEG is strongly epileptic.' The electroencephalogram turned out to be normal, but he prescribed phenobarbital as a precautionary anticonvulsant. That seemed to be effective. I continued to see Kevin every week on one complaint or another, but there were no more seizures until mid-February. We are now into 1979. Then, Mrs. Starke told me, he was doing so well that she stopped the phenobarb for a couple of days, and he went into spasms. That seemed to tell us something.

"But there was worse to come. I think it was the following week. She came into the office looking very unhappy, even frightened. It was only indirectly Kevin. It was her brother Paul, the lawyer in Fayetteville. He'd been thrown while jumping a horse, and killed. And they had found some Dilantin tablets in his pocket. Dilantin is phenytoin, a standard drug in the treatment of epilepsy. The family was doubly stunned. Paul had kept his epilepsy a secret. And— this was what frightened her—wasn't epilepsy an inherited disease? I had to say that it was. Well, she remembered now that her father—he had died last summer—had suffered from shaking spells. I felt distinctly uneasy. I reported to the neurologist what she had told me, and he said he would arrange another consultation. I got his report on March second. He wrote, 'The boy's exam seems good today, with good coordination and no nystagmus and normal fundi. The boy's electroencephalogram is normal. Despite this, I think the most likely explanation for these recurrent episodes is that they are epileptic seizures, and that it would be appropriate to continue him on the phenobarbital . . . [and] that I see him again in one year.' That puzzled me a little. It seemed to be based entirely on brother Paul's epilepsy. Still, a normal EEG does not rule out epilepsy. Normal EEGs are not uncommon between seizures. Also, anticonvulsant therapy tends to diminish EEG abnormalities. So I had to take the report seriously. So did my associates here in the office. I was the physician of record for Kevin, and I saw him on the great majority of his visits. But, of course, I wasn't always here. One or another of my colleagues saw him once in a while. And we often discussed him at staff meetings. None of us felt comfortable about him. Or her. But, as I've said, a doctor can't pick and choose or keep or dismiss his patients. And acceptance of the patient's veracity—a parent's veracity in the case of a baby—is basic to medicine.

"Well, the weekly visits, the weekly dramas, continued. The seizures, however, seemed to be satisfactorily controlled by daily phenobarbital. But that period ended in May. Mrs. Starke reported a series of serious seizures. I decided to get an opinion from another neurologist. It was arranged and done, and I received the results on May thirty-first. The report concluded,

'1. Normal neurological examination. 2. In all probability, this boy does have a seizure disorder on a familial basis. He has had ten episodes and they seem to be correlated with a decrease in his phenobarbital. I would suggest he be continued on phenobarbital and keep the level between 20 and 30 ug/ml. I do not see any reason to do any further diagnostic studies at this time.' As before, the seizures seemed to come under control. Then they flared again. We added Dilantin to the therapy. And with seemingly good results. He was hospitalized in Fayetteville for a day or two with a fever of a hundred and five in July. It seemed to be one of the usual ear, nose, or throat complaints." Dr. Guandolo turned the pages of the chart. "We played the same scene every week. But it was never anything but strange. I mean, it was queer. There would be the frantic phone call, and then the insouciant arrival, and then her account of what had happened, with hardly a touch of concern. And the only abnormality I ever found was an ear infection now and then. There was also another peculiarity. We try to make our little patients feel good about coming here. We give them a present of some sort on every visit—usually a little plastic dinosaur. Once in a while, depending on the complaint, Kevin would come in a bit groggy or lethargic. He would lie like a lump while I examined him. But when I offered him his present he woke right up.

"I talked to the neurologist who had seen Kevin in May, and we decided on another consultation. That was in March of 1980. I got his report on the tenth. It began, 'Kevin's seizure disorder was doing well until about a week ago. At that time, he had seven to nine seizures in one day. His mother says that the seizures consist of passing out and being unresponsive. Then his arms and legs will tremble, and this will last for one to two minutes. . . . On examination, he was alert and responsive. . . .' And here is his conclusion: '1. Normal neurological exam. 2. Seizure disorder. It is very difficult to understand how such a normal child could have so many seizures, but this is possible. The mother is describing generalized tonic-clonic convulsions. I think for the time being I would leave his medications alone.' I quite agreed with that last. Kevin's medications were now phenobarbital, Dilantin, and chloral hydrate. Mrs. Starke had reported that he was often excited at night, and she insisted on having something to help him sleep. My feeling was that his sleeplessness was related to the phenobarbital. It sometimes has that reverse effect. I think it was about this time—the spring of 1980—that Kevin began to develop serious headaches. Mrs. Starke said she was worried, because she knew about headaches. Her husband and her mother-in-law both suffered from migraine. By now, of course, Kevin was talking pretty well. But his mother still did the talking. He would say yes or no, and when she reported his headaches he looked at me and touched his head and said, 'It hurts.' I conferred with the neurologist, and eventually propranolol was added to the list of medications."

Dr. Guandolo sifted through the papers on the table. "Here's a report from another direction," he said. "It came to me from a doctor in the Department of Endocrinology and Metabolism of Children's Hospital National Medical Center. Mrs. Starke and Kevin had shown up there on July eighth. Here's what the report said: 'According to the mother, Kevin missed supper on July 6, 1980, two days prior to my seeing him. The next day, according to her, he vomited all day and had essentially no intake. I saw him about noon, and she reported that he had had no intake. . . . She was concerned because he was becoming lethargic. On examination Kevin was indeed lethargic, somewhat slow in his responses; he gradually became more alert after he had been here about ½ hour and after he had drunk a glass of orange juice. . . . Physical examination was unremarkable. He was not dehydrated. . . . As I mentioned above, Kevin became gradually alert and active after being here about ½ hour. He did vomit once while he was here, but that was while he was in the bathroom with his mother and he could not be observed. . . . I am unsure what is going on with Kevin. . . . Perhaps he has migraine headaches, although in questioning Kevin we could get no indication that he was having a headache while he was here. I do not believe that he has a metabolic disorder causing his vomiting. I am still a little skeptical as to whether he is really sick, although it was clear when we saw him that he was definitely lethargic. It is hard to reconcile the mother's history with a blood glucose of 92 and negative urine ketones.' " Dr. Guandolo returned the paper to the clutter on the table. He said, "Did you notice what he said about the vomiting in the bathroom? That was interesting.

"We had another neurological examination scheduled for August—August sixth. It was the same neurologist as before, and his findings were as before. His conclusion was, 'The nature of his episodes of lethargy and vomiting is still not clear. These could be attacks of migraine. I do not know any way to prove this diagnosis.' And the weekly office visits continued as before. I remember one of the nurses telling me one afternoon that she thought Kevin probably had the biggest collection of plastic dinosaurs in the world. There was one thing that was beginning to seriously bother me. That was the medications he was taking. Even if they were effective—and I wasn't at all sure that they were—they were getting to be too much. I have a note I made in early November of 1981. I noted that Kevin had been receiving phenobarbital for thirty-five months. He had been taking Dilantin for twenty-seven months. And propranolol for nineteen months. I suggested to Mrs. Starke one afternoon that we start tapering off his drugs. She almost panicked. He needed the drugs. Had I forgotten his reaction when he had missed a couple of days? She hadn't, and neither had her husband. Nor had her brother Patrick. She had just had a letter from him. She brought the letter on the next visit. It was typewritten and addressed to 'Dear Sis.' It began with family chat. Then this: 'A note to Dr. Guandolo. Anything I say to him is open to you and Frank. In answer to a few questions he has asked you: My recollection of Kevin's seizure is dim—I imagine because I assumed his seizure disorder had been diagnosed. I do recall that what I saw was pretty much characteristic of an epileptic seizure. Maybe along with rhythmic trembling, a little jerking of the extremities.' A couple of weeks later, just before Christmas, she brought in another letter from Patrick. It included this comment: 'If you and Frank are unhappy and Kevin is rebellious with the setup, environment, neurologist, then maybe you need to have second thoughts. . . . Muddle it over with your friend Dr. Guandolo. I think it's important to try to straighten Kevin out and have him on the proper medications.' There was one more that she shared with me. It was dated February 7, 1982. It ended, 'Our neurological history and then Kevin's. Darn it—try it. It adds up.' I read and reread them. Patrick sounded like a nice, affectionate brother. But he didn't sound like much of a doctor.

"Those letters, the more I thought about them, gave me a little extra push. I had been wanting to talk to Mr. Starke for a good long time, but she always put me off. He was always away, always traveling somewhere—usually abroad. But finally I decided it had to be done; I had to take the initiative. I got his office number and called him up, and he was there, and we arranged to meet here early the following morning. That was March third. He came in at eight-thirty on the dot. He was a quiet, remote sort of man. I began by asking him about Kevin. I hadn't seen him for several days. How was he doing? Starke looked puzzled. What did I mean? Was there something wrong with Kevin? I told him no—nothing new. His seizures and migraine and all the rest seemed under control. Starke stared at me. He looked absolutely flabbergasted. He said he knew that his wife brought Kevin here from time to time. But he had had no idea—he thought it was only for routine baby problems. Now it was my turn to be flabbergasted. I stared at him. I had a feeling that Frank and Laurie were not a very close couple. I thought of those two hundred or more office visits at thirty dollars a visit and four years of expensive drugs—and he knew nothing about it! Well, we finally got straightened out enough to get started, to talk. Kevin had never, to his knowledge, had a seizure or an episode of all-night vomiting or anything like a migraine headache. Or anything but an occasional cold and a few earaches. We got around to Laurie. She *had* majored in English at Virginia. She had worked as a receptionist in a doctor's office, and she had also worked as a bookkeeper at a hospital. She had never attended law school, she had never taken a bar exam, she had never studied Russian history. He himself, of course, was a lawyer, and he was also a student of Russian history. No, he had never had a migraine headache. No, his father-in-law was not an epileptic. Paul? Laurie didn't have a brother named Paul. Nor did she have a brother named Patrick. She was an only child. No, they had never had a sitter named Cindy. Or a neighbor called Dr. Jack. Travel? Yes, he now and then traveled on business, but only in this country. He had never been abroad. We ended up practically reeling. I was bewildered. But I knew I had heard the truth. A few minutes after Starke had left, I telephoned Mrs. Starke. I half expected Cindy to answer the phone, but it was Mrs. Starke. I said that the several consultants and I had decided that Kevin must be hospitalized for a number of in-patient tests, and had to be taken off all medications. She heard me out, and then said, 'Well, I'll have to talk to Frank about that.' I asked her to ask him to call me. She said that wasn't possible. Frank was at a meeting in Tennessee—in Knoxville. But she would be talking to him this evening, and she would call me in the morning. And she did. She said she had told Frank what I wanted to do. She said, 'He almost hit the ceiling. He wants Kevin to stay on his medication. And so does Patrick.' I've forgotten what I said. I've forgotten just how the call ended. It was the first time I had ever heard a cold-blooded lie.

"We now knew the truth about Kevin and Laurie. We knew, at least, that we had been the victims of a sham, a deliberate fabrication at the expense of a little boy. But we didn't know why. It had been puzzling before, and disturbing. Now it was a mystery. And weird almost beyond belief. Then, by an absolute freak of chance, we got a glimmer of light. Gordon Mella—one of my associates—walked into my office one morning a few days after my meeting with Frank Starke. He said, 'Here's something I just happened to come across. I think you'll be interested in it.' He handed me a paper. It was an abstract of an article by an English pediatrician named Roy Meadow that had appeared in the August 13, 1977, issue of *The Lancet*. The title was 'Munchausen Syndrome by Proxy: The Hinterland of Child Abuse.' I read it almost at a glance. I had never heard the name Munchausen. I had never heard of Munchausen's Syndrome. And I certainly had never heard of Munchausen's Syndrome by Proxy. Neither had Dr. Mella. But we were only too familiar with Dr. Meadow's hinterland."

The name Munchausen, as Dr. Guandolo is now indelibly aware, refers to Hieronymus Karl Friedrich, Freiherr von Münchhausen (1720–97), a retired veteran of several European wars, who entertained guests at his estate in Hesse with outrageously absurd but straight-faced accounts of his heroic exploits abroad. These *Lügendichtungen* (or liar's tales) were extracted from the family circle by a onetime friend —a scholar turned thief turned fugitive and expatriate—named Rudolf Erich Raspe (1737–94) in a moment of financial insecurity, and published in England (in 1785) in a book entitled *Baron Munchausen's Narrative of His Marvellous Travels and Campaigns in Russia*, which became (to the baron's embarrassment) one of the most durable best-sellers of all time. In the course of the book's success and long celebrity, the baron's name (in its Anglicized form) evolved into a synonym for the mendacious and far-fetched. Munchausen's Syndrome, as a name, derives from this generic elevation, and was the invention of an English clinician named Richard Asher, who first identified the psychopathological aberration it describes. It was introduced to medicine in an article published in *The Lancet* in 1951. "Here," Asher's landmark "Munchausen's Syndrome" began, "is described a common syndrome which most doctors have seen, but about which little has been written. Like the famous Baron von Munchausen, the persons affected have always travelled widely; and their stories, like those attributed to him, are both dramatic and untruthful. Accordingly, the syndrome is respectfully dedicated to the baron, and named after him." The article continues:

> The patient showing the syndrome is admitted to hospital with apparent acute illness supported by a plausible and dramatic history. Usually his story is largely made up of falsehoods; he is found to have attended, and deceived, an astounding number of other hospitals. . . . It is almost impossible to be certain of the diagnosis at first, and it requires a bold

casualty officer to refuse admission. . . . It must be recognized that these patients are often quite ill, although their illness is shrouded by duplicity and distortion. . . . Often a real organic lesion from the past has left some genuine physical signs which the patient uses. . . . Most cases resemble organic emergencies. Well-known varieties are: 1. The acute abdominal type. . . . 2. The haemorrhagic type, who specialise in bleeding from lungs or stomach. . . . 3. The neurological type, presenting with paroxysmal headache, loss of consciousness, or peculiar fits. The most remarkable feature of the syndrome is the apparent senselessness of it. Unlike the malingerer, who may gain a definite end, these patients often seem to gain nothing except the discomfiture of unnecessary investigations or operations. Their initial tolerance to the more brutish hospital measures is remarkable, yet they commonly discharge themselves after a few days with operation wounds scarcely healed, or intravenous drips still running. . . . Sometimes the motive is never clearly ascertained, but . . . one of the following mechanisms may be involved: 1. A desire to be the center of interest and attention. . . . 2. A grudge against doctors and hospitals. . . . 3. A desire for drugs. 4. A desire to escape from the police. . . . 5. A desire to get free board and lodgings for the night. . . . Supplementing these scanty motives, there probably exists some strange twist of personality. Perhaps most cases are hysterics, schizophrenics, masochists, or psychopaths of some kind.

If those afflicted with Munchausen's Syndrome are often driven by masochistic need, the perpetrators of Munchausen's Syndrome by Proxy would seem to be in need of sadistic satisfaction. The stratagems that both employ, however, are basically the same. "Some patients," Meadow noted in his elaboration of Munchausen's Syndrome into Munchausen's Syndrome by Proxy, "consistently produce false stories and fabricate evidence, so causing themselves needless hospital investigations and operations. Here are described parents who, by falsification, caused their children innumerable harmful hospital procedures. . . . Doctors dealing with young children rely on the parents' recollection of the history. The doctor accepts that history, albeit sometimes with a pinch of salt, and it forms the cornerstone of subsequent investigation and management of the child. A case is reported in which over a period of six years, the parents systematically provided fictitious information about their child's symptoms, tampered with the urine specimens to produce false results and interfered with hospital observations. . . . The case is compared with another child who was intermittently given toxic doses of salt which again led to massive investigation in three different centres. . . . During the investigation of both these children, we came to know the mothers well. They were very pleasant people to deal with, coöperative, and appreciative of good medical care. . . . These cases are a reminder that at times doctors must accept the parents' history and indeed the laboratory findings with more than usual scepticism. We may teach, and I believe should teach, that mothers are always right; but at the same time we must recognize that when mothers are wrong they can be terribly wrong."

The caution and unease with which Meadow sounds this warning is not hard to understand. His experience of a cruelly mendacious mother, like that of Dr. Guandolo and his colleagues, discovers dangerous territory. "One of the essential attributes of the physician must be a readiness to accept the patient's story," E. Clarke and S. C. Melnick declared in a discussion of Munchausen's Syndrome in the *American Journal of Medicine*, in 1958, "and if we should ever cast doubts upon the veracity of his statements, the whole structure of clinical medicine would be undermined."

The rest of Dr. Guandolo's account of his lengthy introduction to what he likes to call, using a phrase of Dr. Asher's, Neurologica Diabolica I heard over lunch. Dr. Mella joined us. The cuisine, at their suggestion, was Chinese, and they ate, stylishly and gracefully, with chopsticks and refrained from comment when I chose a knife and fork. "Meadow was a revelation," Dr. Guandolo said. "An awful revelation. His mothers were practically monsters." He ate a puff of shrimp. "But it was also comforting. He told us, at least, that we were dealing with something known. We weren't totally in the dark. It had happened before. In fact, as we know now, many times before. So we knew the nature of the problem. It wasn't Kevin. It was his mother. We decided for the moment to say nothing to her. It was best that she didn't know what we knew. Kevin came first. We wanted him in the hospital. We wanted him off all medications, and that could be done best there. And we wanted him away from his mother, so we could see for ourselves. We didn't believe in those seizures or those migraines or those vomitings and all the rest. But we wanted to be absolutely sure. I won't go into all the details, but we managed to hospitalize him. He was watched and thoroughly examined by a team at Children's Hospital.

He came off drugs without incident, and the indicated tests were all negative. Then we turned our attention to Mrs. Starke. The time had come to confront her. She would be taken aside when she came to visit Kevin. The confrontation team was composed of the neurologist who had seen her and Kevin, a child psychiatrist, a staff pediatrician who was Kevin's attending physician, and a resident. It was decided that I step aside and remain neutral. That way, I could maintain a cordial relationship with her. It must have been a dramatic meeting. She was told gently but firmly that her fantasy world was detrimental to both Kevin and herself, and that she needed psychiatric help. The possibility of a child-abuse citation was mentioned. She wilted. That was on April second. I talked to her on the telephone the following day. First to Starke, and then to her. She was soft-spoken, contrite, and sobbing. She said, 'I can't see you for a few days. But, oh, Dr. G., thanks!' I thought she was sincere."

"I wonder," Dr. Mella said.

"I know," Dr. Guandolo said. "When I talked with her again, she said, 'I don't know who that other person was. Maybe it was Gertrude the Witch.' "

"She *was* a kind of witch," Dr. Mella said. "I thought she was very clever and persuasive. If she had been a drug addict, she could have got drugs from any of us. I don't see her as actually wicked. I think she was a medical buff. She loved her visits to the office. I never saw her in any hurry to leave. It gave her some kind of satisfaction to be here. Kevin was her ticket of admission."

"I agree," Dr. Guandolo said. "But I think we also agree on something else. She programmed Kevin to

34

be ill. She needed a dependent. Her husband certainly wasn't one. He kept everybody at arm's length. She bound Kevin to her by constant mothering and constant medical care. We'll never know any more. The Starkes moved away later on that year—back home to North Carolina, I think. She had a few sessions with a psychiatrist before they left, but I don't think he learned much of anything. I made a report to the Montgomery County Family Services office here in Maryland, but if they ever made an investigation they didn't tell me about it. After the family moved, I also reported the case to the appropriate state office in North Carolina. I suggested that any doctor approached by Mrs. Starke and her little boy be advised to get in touch with me. No one ever has."

"And that was the end of it?" I asked.

"Yes," Dr. Guandolo said. "That was it. But I sometimes think of something Kevin said not long before they left." He and Dr. Mella exchanged a glance. "Mrs. Starke continued to bring him into the office. Once in a while. And mostly for plausible reasons. This time, he had one of his earaches. He really did suffer, off and on, from earaches. I wrote out a prescription for an antibiotic and handed it to her. Kevin saw what it was. He grinned, and said, 'Oh, boy—I get medicine.'"

[*1986*]

# Cinnabar

A mong the several regular patients who consulted Dr. Joyce Wallace, an internist, at her office on West Twelfth Street, off Seventh Avenue, on Friday morning, March 19, 1979, was a drop-in whom I'll call Laura McBride. Mrs. McBride was forty-three years old and a widow with three teenage daughters. She was, she told Dr. Wallace, an art conservator by profession, and she did her work at home, just around the corner, on West Thirteenth Street. She had come to Dr. Wallace at the suggestion of her gynecologist. The gynecologist had noted during a recent routine examination that her hemoglobin level was low. The gynecologist thought that this decrease was probably due to heavy menstrual bleeding, but it might reflect a developing anemia, and she advised her to see an internist for a complete physical examination. Mrs. McBride hesitated. But that, she said, was only partly why she was here. She had seen the gynecologist in December. She had felt perfectly well, and had kept putting off the suggested visit to an internist. She was here today because for the past three weeks she had been having pains. They came and went. Pains in her stomach, and a burning pain lower down. She touched an area known to physiology as the left upper quadrant of the abdomen. She said she also seemed to be tired most of the time. She couldn't do her regular exercises. Her muscles ached, and she had occasional dizzy spells. And everything seemed to irritate her, especially her children.

Dr. Wallace observed her patient. She was tall and slim and dark-haired, young-looking for her age, and she appeared to be in good health. Dr. Wallace began the standard physical examination. All the usual signs and systems were normal—all but one. The spleen was palpable. Dr. Wallace could feel the tip of it. That was abnormal but in no way definitive. She stopped and considered. There was nothing remarkable about any of Mrs. McBride's complaints. They could all very well have been functional in origin. But somehow she didn't think they were. Mrs. McBride just didn't impress her as a neurotic type. An instinct told her that those pains and aches, the dizzy spells and the fatigue, the irritability and the myalgia had some organic root. The gynecologist had suspected anemia. Dr. Wallace drew some samples of Mrs. McBride's blood. She asked her to bring in a stool sample. She made an appointment to see her in four days' time, on the following Tuesday.

The results of the blood tests came through. They powerfully confirmed the gynecologist's concern. Mrs. McBride showed a hemoglobin level of 10.3 grams per deciliter. The normal range is from 14 to 16. Her hematocrit reading was 30.7 percent. Normal is from 45 to 50. A third test revealed that Mrs. McBride's production of new red blood cells was higher than normal. This clearly indicated that her body was attempting to compensate for her falling hemoglobin level. All these findings pointed to an iron-deficiency anemia. A further test, however, demolished that explanation. Her iron level and her iron-binding capacity were both normal. Could she be losing blood through internal bleeding? But the stool tests ruled that out. There was no suggestion of blood in her stool. When Mrs. McBride arrived for her Tuesday appointment, Dr. Wallace questioned her about other possible sources of blood loss. Had she been vomiting? No. Had she noticed any blood in her urine? No. Were her menses normal? Yes. Dr. Wallace drew another sample of blood, for another round of tests, and arranged to see her again on Thursday. On Thursday morning, Dr. Wallace had the results of the new blood tests. Mrs. McBride's hemoglobin level had dropped to 9.7 and her hematocrit reading had gone to 28.9. Her symptoms, moreover, had intensified. Her abdominal pains, she told Dr. Wallace, were now cramps—frequent, colicky cramps. Also, she didn't seem to have any strength, and she was often out of breath. Dr. Wallace was puzzled, but more puzzled than alarmed. She decided against any attempt at symptomatic treatment. She drew another sample of blood, asked for another stool sample, and made an appointment for Saturday.

By the time Mrs. McBride arrived for her Saturday appointment, Dr. Wallace had received a report on the blood drawn two days before. Mrs. McBride's hemoglobin level had fallen again, to 9.1. Her hematocrit reading was 28.8. Dr. Wallace began to feel uneasy. "Before my eyes, before my very eyes, she was losing blood," she said. "But where was it going? There was no blood in her stool. There was no blood in her urine. She wasn't vomiting. There was no strong evidence of hemolysis, or early breakage of the red cell. I thought; I racked my brains. Her symptoms were nonspecific. No help there. Then I remembered medical school. I remembered they used to say, 'Look at the blood smear.' Medical school is sometimes right. So I prepared some blood and put it under the microscope. And I saw something. The red blood cells were spotted. I saw the blue marks that we call basophilic stippling. About 40 percent of the red blood cells were stippled. Now I knew something. Stippling suggests toxicity. Her red blood cells were being destroyed. It wasn't certain. It wasn't specific. Stippling occurs in several diseases. But I thought, What does this woman do? Answer: She is an art conservator, a restorer. She works in art. Art materials are chemicals. She works with chemicals. Paint is a chemical. Paint! Lead poisoning! I had never seen a case of lead poisoning in an adult. But I believed I had one now. Her symptoms began to have some meaning. The colicky cramps, the fatigue, the irritability—all those are symptoms of lead poisoning. What to do?

"I told Mrs. McBride what I thought, what I suspected. I said that if my presumptive diagnosis was correct, the source of her illness was almost certainly something in her workroom, her studio. The first thing to do was to remove her from that source of contamination. I told her to stop working, stay out of the workroom, close it off. My reasoning, of course, was that if she avoided the focus of contamination, avoided continued exposure, her body could begin to excrete lead. Excretion of lead is a slow process, but I hoped she would soon be showing some improvement. I told her to get plenty of rest—bed rest. We would keep in touch. I would want a regular supply of blood, to continue with the tests, to follow any changes in her blood chemistry. I also said I would want to visit her workroom. I would call and make a date. I told her what I could that would make her comfortable, and she left. Now I wanted advice. The first thing Monday morning, I called the Department of Health, and told them I had a case of suspected lead poisoning. They gave me the name of a Dr. Alf Fischbein, at Mt. Sinai Medical Center. They said that Mt. Sinai was a center for clinical research in lead poisoning, and that Dr. Fischbein was the leading investigator there."

Lead is one of some twenty thousand chemicals in more or less common use today which are known to be more or less toxic when touched, ingested, or inhaled. Most of these are of recent, or twentieth-century, origin, and the toxic potentialities of most of this group—individually or in infinite combination or interaction—are still poorly understood. There is no such uncertainty about the pernicious powers of lead. Lead has been known and used by man since the earliest hours of civilization, and it was one of the first chemical materials to be recognized as hazardous to health. It seems to have been known to the Greek poet and physician Nicander in the second pre-Christian century. A passage in his clinico-poetical treatise "Alexipharmaca" opens with the line "The harmful cerussa, that most noxious thing." Cerussa is ceruse, or the pigment called white lead. Galen (circa A.D. 150) was sufficiently familiar with the noxious side of lead to warn against its use in water pipes.

Most instances of lead poisoning are, and always have been, among miners and workers in the trades and industries, but lead has also had a sinister affinity for workers in the arts. Bernardino Ramazzini, the seventeenth-century Italian clinician and pioneer in the field of occupational disease, was the first to observe and record this connection. "What city or town is there," he writes in his *De Morbis Artificum Diatriba*, "in which men do not follow the potter's craft, the oldest of all the arts? Now when they need roasted or calcined lead for glazing their pots, they grind the lead in marble vessels. . . . During this process, or again when they use tongs to daub the pots with molten lead before putting them into the furnace, their mouths, nostrils, and the whole body take in the lead poison that has been melted and dissolved in water; hence they are soon attacked by grievous maladies. . . . Painters, too, are attacked by various ailments. . . . It very seldom happens that painters look florid or healthy, though they usually paint the portraits of other people to look handsomer or more florid than they really are. I have observed that nearly all the painters whom I know . . . are sickly; and if one reads the lives of painters it will be seen that they are by no means long-lived, especially those who were most distinguished. We read that Raphael of Urbino, the famous painter, was snatched from life in the very flower of his youth. . . . Their sedentary life and melancholic temperament may be partly to blame . . . but for their liability to disease there is a more immediate cause, I mean the materials of the colors they handle and smell constantly, such as red lead, cinnabar, white lead. . . . Moreover, painters when at work wear dirty clothes smeared with paint, so that their mouths and noses inevitably breathe tainted air; this penetrates to the seat of the animal spirits, enters by the breathing passages the abode of the blood, disturbs the economy of the natural functions." More recent observers have shared Ramazzini's conception of the artist's hygienic innocence. It has been suggested that it was lead poisoning, not schizophrenia or syphilis, that mysteriously disturbed the economy of Goya's natural functions in his middle age, and that it also accounted for the near-insanity that dogged van Gogh for many years. Both painters were partial to white lead and to the heavily leaded Naples yellow, and van Gogh was on at least one occasion seen to actually eat some paint.

Contemporary workers in the arts and crafts are generally aware of the toxicity of lead, and many now avoid the use of lead-containing materials, but the indifferent work habits that Ramazzini noted and that van Gogh so peculiarly exemplified are not yet a thing of the past, and lead poisoning, as Laura McBride can ruefully testify, still occurs in the studio. Indeed, it occurs sufficiently often to have persuaded Dr. Michael McCann, president of the Center for Occupational Hazards, to include in his authoritative 1979 handbook *Artist Beware* (along with the most lethal modern solvents, thinners, cements, and fixatives) seventeen warning references to lead.

Lead poisoning was often on Dr. Wallace's mind over Saturday and Sunday. She was concerned about the McBride children. They, too, might have been exposed to whatever it was that had poisoned their mother. Children are more sensitive to lead poisoning than adults. From her reading she remembered a case of lead poisoning in a woman and her two young children. The source of the poisoning was traced to lead in a ceramic pitcher bought in Mexico. As the two children became more and more ill, the mother, with therapeutic intent, fed them more and more fresh orange juice—served in the toxic pitcher. The mother recovered, but both children suffered permanent brain damage.

On Monday morning, a moment after her call to the Health Department, Dr. Wallace put in a call to Mt. Sinai and Dr. Fischbein. She told him what she knew and what she suspected. Dr. Fischbein listened and considered and informally confirmed her informal diagnosis. He proposed some further, more definitive tests. He said he would send her by hand a couple of specially processed, guaranteed-lead-free containers for samples of blood and urine. They discussed Mrs. McBride's profession and agreed that a visit to her studio was imperative. They would meet there as soon as Dr. Wallace could make the arrangements. Dr. Wallace hung up, and then called Mrs. McBride. She wanted to see her for some more blood and urine samples, and she also wanted to see her children. Although they seemed to be in normal health, she wanted to analyze their blood. Just in case. The containers arrived from Dr. Fischbein, and Mrs. McBride and her children came in. The samples were taken and dispatched. It was arranged that Dr. Wallace and Dr. Fischbein would visit Mrs. McBride's studio on Friday afternoon. The results of the several tests would be in by then. They were. Mrs. McBride's blood showed a lead level of 72 micrograms per deciliter of whole blood. Normal is around 10. Her children's blood tests were normal. That, if there had been much doubt, sharpened the focus on Mrs. McBride's studio.

Mrs. McBride's house was a three-story brownstone, with an English basement. She showed the two doctors into her studio. It was a small room on the parlor (or first) floor, in the rear. There was one window. Closed. The studio had been designed and used by her late husband. He was an art dealer, but he knew quite a lot about art restoring. As a matter of fact, it was from him that she had learned her skills. She ordinarily worked on assignment from dealers, but her current project was an ancient Peruvian tapestry that her husband had purchased several years before his death. It was her understanding that it had been found in a tomb of the Chancay period. It was dated between A.D. 1000 and 1500. The tapestry was on her worktable. It was heavy and frayed and made of wool, with an abstract, geometrical design in tan, red, and brown. The brown areas were the restored parts. Mrs. McBride described her procedure. She had first cleaned the tapestry with a detergent. That had brought back much of the original color. She had begun work in early December. After the cleaning, she had touched up the brown areas with a water-based paint solution. She prepared the paint herself, using a pigment that her husband had acquired along with the tapestry—a pigment that had also been found in the Chancay tomb. She had applied the paint with a feather brush. When the paint was dry, she brushed it to an even texture and then blew off any residue. Worn areas of the tapestry were repaired with needle and thread.

Dr. Wallace and Dr. Fischbein exchanged a glance. Dr. Fischbein's expression was almost a grimace. Mrs. McBride's work habits were practically a model of insouciance. Brushing the newly painted fabric would raise a cloud of dust. Blowing off the residue would raise more. Working on a painted fabric with needle and thread would involve wetting the thread with her tongue. There was a big ashtray on the worktable: Mrs. McBride smoked while she worked. That brought her fingers often to her mouth. Dr. Fischbein mentioned ventilation. Was there a fan, or did she work with the window open? Neither. She kept the window closed to save on heat. This wasn't a rented apartment. She owned the house and paid the heating bills. Dr. Wallace asked if she knew the nature of the ancient pigment she was using. Oh, yes. It was cinnabar. Dr.

Wallace and Dr. Fischbein exchanged another glance—a glance, this time, of puzzlement. Cinnabar is mercuric sulfide, and mercuric sulfide (contrary to Ramazzini's understanding) is not a particularly toxic substance. Unlike lead, it is largely insoluble in tissue fluids, and whether inhaled or ingested passes more or less harmlessly through the body. In any event, the signs and symptoms of mercury poisoning are very different from those of lead. Dr. Fischbein asked if cinnabar was the only chemical that Mrs. McBride used in her work. Mrs. McBride said that to the best of her knowledge it was. She added that she certainly didn't use any form of lead.

Dr. Wallace and Dr. Fischbein took a final look around the studio. It told them nothing. They both found it hard to believe that Mrs. McBride's illness was not related to her work. Still, as they both well knew, the literature of lead poisoning contains some bizarre chapters. Dr. Fischbein could recall a case in which the victim was also afflicted with geophagia. Geophagia is a compulsion to eat earth. The victim's usual grazing ground was the shoulder of a highway, the soil of which was found to be rich in lead from years of gasoline fumes. Nevertheless, before they left, Dr. Fischbein asked for and was given a sample of Mrs. McBride's husband's cinnabar and a snippet of the tapestry.

Mrs. McBride continued, on the advice of both doctors, to rest in bed. There was increasingly nothing much else she could do. Her condition continued to worsen. In addition to the colicky cramps, the shortness of breath, and the darkening irritability, she now showed signs of neurological disease. Her legs from hip to ankle were weak and getting weaker. Dr. Wallace and Dr. Fischbein continued to monitor her blood. Discontinuing work in her studio had failed to rebalance her blood chemistry. Her hemoglobin level, instead of rising, continued to fall—from 9.1 to 8.7 to 7.7. This last, together with the increasing severity of her symptoms, was definitely alarming, and it was decided that a series of blood transfusions was indicated. That was on Sunday, April 4. Dr. Wallace admitted her to St. Vincent's Hospital, a block or two from her home. Over the next several days, Mrs. McBride was given a total of three units of packed red blood cells. There was an almost immediate improvement in certain signs and symptoms. Her disposition brightened and her strength began to return. Her hemoglobin level gratifyingly climbed to 10.5. She was discharged to resume her rest at home. Her hemoglobin level remained stable for a week or more. Then it again declined. On April 20, it dropped to 9.9. Another blood-lead-level study was done. The result was a reading of 127 micrograms per deciliter of whole blood—over twelve times the normal level and three times the acceptable level. Three days later, on April 23, her hemoglobin level had fallen again, to 9.3. Urinary and other tests also showed an increasingly morbid presence of lead. But it was the blood lead level that most impressed Dr. Fischbein. It was one of the highest he had ever seen. He recommended, and Dr. Wallace concurred, that a course of chelation therapy be started at once.

———

Mrs. McBride was readmitted to St. Vincent's Hospital on April 26 for a course of chelation therapy. Chelation involves the administration of a drug that has the power to combine with—to bind and secure—a metal and remove it from the body by excretion in the urine. There are three chelating agents in more or less general use: BAL (British antilewisite); a derivative of penicillin called penicillamine; and calcium disodium ethylenediamine tetra-acetic acid. $CaNa_2$-EDTA, as the last is commonly called, was the agent chosen for Mrs. McBride. The dosage was 1 gram in a solution of 250 milliliters of 5 percent dextrose twice a day for five days. Serious side effects—among them heart irregularities and impaired kidney function—are not uncommon in chelation therapy, and Mrs. McBride's reactions were closely monitored, including a daily urinalysis to measure the amount of lead excreted. Her tolerance of $CaNa_2$-EDTA was generally satisfactory, and ten days after the completion of the course her blood lead level had fallen to 74 micrograms per deciliter of whole blood, and her symptoms—abdominal pain, muscular aches, and irritability—had notably eased. She was discharged from the hospital on May 6.

The results of chelation therapy can be, and often are, misleading. Three weeks later, on May 27, a routine examination revealed that Mrs. McBride's blood lead level had again increased—to 84 micrograms per deciliter of whole blood—and her aches and pains and bad temper had returned. This, to Dr. Wallace and Dr. Fischbein, was disappointing but not particularly alarming. It seemed to indicate that Mrs. McBride's accumulation of lead had been greater than they had assumed. This accumulation, stored in her bones and soft tissues, was being released into her blood by the effects of chelation. It was decided that a second course of chelation therapy should be done, and on June 25 she was admitted once more to St. Vincent's Hospital. Her blood lead level at admission was 103 micrograms per deciliter of whole blood. A second course of chelation with $CaNa_2$-EDTA was commenced. This series, like the first, was without untoward incident, and her improvement was prompt and impressive. She was again discharged, to be followed as an outpatient by Dr. Wallace. In early September, after almost a year of travail and treatment, a final round of tests showed her condition to be normal—hemoglobin, hematocrit, and blood lead level.

Meanwhile, during those weeks of spring and summer, as Mrs. McBride was hospitalized and discharged and hospitalized again, Dr. Fischbein was deeply engaged in trying to determine the source and focus of her trouble. The first step in this determination was an analysis of the red pigment known to Mrs. McBride as cinnabar. The study, which involved such procedures as polarized-light microscopy and X-ray powder diffraction, was directed by a mineralogist named Arthur N. Rohl. It showed that the powder was indeed cinnabar—was mercuric sulfide. A close analysis of the analysis, however, suggested to Dr. Rohl a hint of the presence of red lead. On the basis of this suspicion, the powder was subjected to the finer scrutiny of electrothermal atomic absorption. The result confirmed his suspicion. The powder contained 8.9 parts lead per thousand, or about 1 percent, and the fabric had a lead concentration of 380 parts per million.

"That was a high concentration," Dr. Fischbein says. "It was certainly high enough to account for the severity of her poisoning. It was also a big relief to us to find the source in the cinnabar. Cinnabar was the only clue we had. But cinnabar isn't lead. Cinnabar is mercuric sulfide. So the next question was: Where did the red lead come from? That was a question that neither Dr. Wallace nor I was qualified to answer. But we inquired around and came up with the names of two anthropologists familiar with the Peruvian culture of the Chancay period. They were Junius B. Bird, of the American Museum of Natural History, now deceased, and Heather Lechtman, of the Massachusetts Institute of Technology. We talked to them both. Could the lead have been added originally to the cinnabar as a preservative? Could it have been added to enhance the color? The answer to both questions was no. Lead was not known to have been used for either purpose in the Chancay period. Well! Then how did the lead contamination come about? We have no certain answer. But we have a hypothesis, a possibility. If the cinnabar was of the same period as the tapestry, as the history of Mrs. McBride's pigment would indicate, it would have a certain antiquarian value. But cinnabar is sold by weight, and it is not a particularly heavy substance. Suppose, then, that somewhere along the devious route from the Chancay tomb to the New York studio one of the several hands through which it passed added a little red lead to make the transaction a little more profitable. There doesn't seem to be any more satisfactory answer. At any rate, it satisfied Dr. Wallace, and it satisfied me, too. It's hard to believe that the contamination was accidental. And if Mrs. McBride had had a somewhat better understanding of the hygiene of her craft it is probable that no harm would have been done."

[*1986*]

# The Poker Room

I went up to Halifax, the capital and principal city of Nova Scotia, and had a talk with Dr. Thomas J. Marrie, professor of medicine and head of the Division of Infectious Diseases of Dalhousie University School of Medicine there, about a recent case whose resolution gave him perhaps more satisfaction than any of the several other medical perplexities with which he has been confronted. One reason, I gathered, for this good feeling was that he sensed the probable nature of the problem within a matter of hours, and had then only to confirm it. Another was that its confirmation was achieved with equal dispatch.

"Well, yes," Dr. Marrie told me. "I guess that's about right." We were sitting in his office in the Victoria

General Hospital complex, a tiny room made smaller by an encirclement of filing cabinets, bookshelves, and a computer and its attendant paraphernalia, but with a big window that opened on a resuscitating expanse of bright blue summer sky. Dr. Marrie is in his middle forties and a native of Newfoundland, of distant French ancestry. His surname was originally Marie, but, Newfoundland being as generally British as Quebec is French, it was soon Englished into its present somewhat Scottish look. He is a tall man of athletic build, with dark brown hair and a strong nose, and could probably pass for French. "Of course," he went on, "I had a certain advantage, a rather special advantage: I had a hunch, a very good hunch, that this was something I had seen before."

He gave a little shrug. "We'll go into that later. The outbreak you're interested in occurred a couple of years ago—in March of 1987. I came into the picture on March fifteenth. One of my colleagues here, a gastroenterologist, called me that morning. He had a patient on referral from a family physician in Digby, about a hundred miles from here. The patient was a black man, thirty-five years old. I'll call him Kenneth Andrews. He'd been sick about a week, since March eighth, with chills and fever, chest pain, and a severe headache. A chest X ray showed evidence of pneumonia. Well, the pneumonias are a special interest of mine. My colleague thought I might like to take a look at Mr. Andrews. I saw him that afternoon. He was sick, all right. He was sweating profusely, and acting a little strange. I asked him some questions, but he seemed suspicious and evasive. About all I learned was that he had been up here in Halifax on a visit

54

several weeks earlier. I looked at his X rays, and the evidence of pneumonia was certainly there. There were two rounded opacities that were very suggestive. But he was being treated with appropriate antibiotics, and I had other patients to see and students to teach. I didn't give him a lot more thought.

"Two or three days went by. I happened to be on our rotating consultation service that month. That meant that I saw, as a consultant, most of the patients who were admitted into our hospital complex with what appeared to be an infectious disease. One of these patients brought Kenneth Andrews back to mind. That was, I think, March eighteenth. This patient was another black man, aged forty-five, whom I'll call Charles Barton. He presented with very much the same symptoms as Andrews. A chest X ray showed a very similar pneumonia. The only difference was that he wasn't from Digby—wasn't from out of town at all. He lived here in Halifax. Another couple of days went by. And another black man turned up with the same presenting picture, including a notable chest X ray. I'll call him Peter Curran. Curran lived in Halifax, too. The only difference here was his age. He was in his seventies. Well, Curran coming on top of Barton, and Barton coming on top of Andrews, made me stop and think. I don't mean because they were all black. That doesn't mean anything here in Halifax. We've had a considerable black population—and a pretty well integrated black population—for well over a hundred years. This was one of the important terminals for the famous Underground Railroad that sneaked so many black people out of the American slave states before and during the American Civil War. Actually, once I stopped to think, I didn't have to do much thinking. All three men had the same suggestive symptoms, particularly the terrible headaches. And the chest X rays were practically definitive. This was a disease I was only too familiar with. This was an outbreak of Q fever."

Q fever is in several respects as peculiar as its name. It manifests, in fact, a consortium of qualities that are shared by few other diseases. It's one of a handful of diseases of international incidence whose existence was first observed in Australia. It was recognized there, in 1935, by E. H. Derrick, a physician associated with the Queensland Health Department, who was investigating an outbreak of prostrating fever among workers in a Brisbane slaughterhouse. Derrick announced his find with a diffidence uncommon in medical science. He *thought* he was seeing a new pathological entity, but he wasn't entirely sure, and he gave expression to this uncertainty by calling it Q (for "query") fever. (It is sometimes erroneously supposed that Derrick, following a more conventional procedure, named his new disease for Queensland, its place of origin.) The originality of his discovery was confirmed by the identification of the causative organism as a hitherto unknown member of the bacterial tribe *Rickettsiae*. A fellow Australian, the Nobel laureate Sir MacFarlane Burnet, is generally credited with this identification. As it happened, however, Burnet's work was duplicated, independently and coincidentally, by the American bacteriologist Herald Rea Cox, at Nine Mile Creek, in Montana. Q fever was at one time known in the American West as Nine Mile Creek fever.

The organism, after some hesitation, was eventually given the name *Coxiella burnetii*, in commemoration of its far-flung elucidation.

The *Rickettsiase* comprise a very small group of microorganisms that are pathogenic to man, but they include the causes of such ferocious afflictions as epidemic typhus, scrub typhus, and Rocky Mountain spotted fever. Q fever is not a member of this unpleasant company. It is violently abrupt in onset and acutely painful, with a characteristic headache that is often described as all but intolerable, but its course is usually unthreatening (and readily blocked by antibiotics), and though there may be subsequent troublesome complications, it is only rarely fatal. It is, on the other hand, one of the most infectious of all diseases. It has been noted that a single viable organism is enough to cause an infection. The rickettsial fevers in general are transmitted to man by the bite of an infected tick, louse, or mite. Q fever is an exception. Like such notoriously contagious diseases as influenza, measles, mumps, whooping cough, the common cold, and (though now seemingly banished from the earth) smallpox, it is contracted by inhalation. Because it chooses this portal of entry, it most commonly finds its way to the lungs. But even in this it stands distinctively alone. In influenza and its viral kindred, the infecting organism is transmitted by the sneezes, coughs, and nose-blowings of its victims. Q fever is not transmitted from man to man. It is a zoonosis, a disease of animals, principally certain livestock (goats, sheep, and cattle), in which man is only accidentally a victim. *C. burnetii* enters its preferred animal host through the bite of a harboring tick, and then moves to perpetuate itself by way of the excreta of its victim. It is present in the feces, in the urine, in the milk, and, particularly, in the placental materials of parturition. When it thus emerges from its animal victim, it is an organism of long life and rugged constitution. In this form, in which it abides between hosts, it can survive for many months in almost any environment. It is resistant to both moisture and desiccation. It has been found, alive and still pathogenic, in milk kept (for experimental purposes) at room temperature for three years or more. Contaminated manure broadcast in barn or pasture or along the road has been implicated in several considerable Q fever outbreaks. One of these, involving more than three hundred people, occurred in Switzerland in 1983, and was traced to the frequent passage of sheep down an Alpine valley road. Another outbreak was reported in Wales in 1981.

The chief victims of Q fever are, as might be supposed, people who live and work with livestock—cattlemen, dairy farmers, sheepherders, sheepshearers, veterinarians, meat packers and processors, and (as in Brisbane in 1935) slaughterhouse workers. People who handle such livestock products as hides and wool are also seriously at risk. Nor is that all. The threat of Q fever is now seen as by no means confined to the countryside or to the products of animal husbandry. The animal reservoir of the disease most probably embraces the whole of the animal kingdom, including, as Dr. Marrie's experience has increasingly shown, some of man's closest companions.

Dr. Marrie touched a switch, and the screen went dark. He removed the last slide from the projector and put it in its wheel-like holder. We were in a kind of viewing room just around the corner from his office, where we had been looking at the chest X rays of Kenneth Andrews, the first of the Q fever patients. One roentgenograph had been taken upon his admission, the other a day later. In both, the opacities indicative of Q fever pneumonitis, dully white against the dark of the lung fields, and about the size of a silver dollar, were clearly apparent even to me.

"I could show you some others," Dr. Marrie said, "but those were the best. Some of the best I ever saw." I followed him out to the hall, and we walked back to his office. "I have to say I was suspicious from almost the first. Certainly from when I saw Andrews's second-day pictures. The Barton and Curran X rays simply confirmed it. To my satisfaction, at least. But, of course, that wasn't enough. There is a definitive test to determine the presence in the blood of antibodies to the *C. burnetii* organism. Samples were taken from Andrews and the two others, and when the results came through they were positive for Q fever. I might mention that the strain of *C. burnetii* whose antigens we use is homegrown. That is, it's North American, not Australian. It's called the Nine Mile strain. But I'm getting ahead of myself. By the time we had those test results, we had a great deal more to think about. Andrews's case, as I've said, was interesting. I'm interested in the pneumonias and I'm interested in Q fever. But it wasn't until I saw the second case, and then the third, that I got really interested. There was something different going on here. Q fever is not an everyday disease. Three cases so close together constituted, in epidemiological terms, a cluster, and a cluster suggests an outbreak. An outbreak suggests a common source, a link of some sort. I remember talking to Peter Curran. I asked him did he happen to know a man named Charles Barton. He said, yes, he knew him. They were good friends. I said, did he happen to know a man named Kenneth Andrews. Sure, he knew him, too. They all played poker together. He and Charlie Barton played together all the time. Andrews sat in whenever he happened to be in town. Then I asked him where they usually played. Did they play in any particular place? Yeah, sure, they had a regular place. They always played at Tom Dalton's. He had a house over on Munich Street. There was a game going on there every day. Well! So I went back and talked to Kenneth Andrews. When I talked to him before, he had acted rather strange and evasive. He was still evasive, but I eventually got him to talk. What was bothering him, I finally realized, was his fear of getting into trouble: he somehow had the idea that playing poker was against the law here in Halifax. When I reassured him, he opened up, and he had plenty to say. He confirmed everything that Curran had told me. The poker game was practically nonstop. There was a whole crowd that played there pretty regularly. There was only one game, one table. The table seated seven. Those who weren't playing stood around and watched, and waited for one of the players to drop out. One way or another, I pieced together a list of the regulars at the game. There were twenty-eight of them.

"Q fever is not a nationally reportable disease here or in the States. It is in Australia, but not here. That means that I had no obligation to do any more than treat the patients who came into the hospital. It was

not a public-health problem. But I was interested. I
wanted to know the whole story of the outbreak. And
it really was an outbreak by then. I had a new case on
my list—Thomas Dalton, the owner of the house on
Munich Street and the proprietor of the game. He was
also black, and forty-eight years old. That wasn't all.
There were other poker players involved. There was a
William Evans, forty-five, also black. Then a twenty-
eight-year-old white girl. She worked in a bank. Then
another black male, forty-nine. Then two more white
women, one of them fifty-three and the other thirty-
nine. The younger woman was Dalton's ex-wife. Then
came another black man I'll call Raymond Kelly. He
was sixty years old and arrived at the hospital in a
coma, and died a couple of hours later. He had Q fever, but he also had some underlying problems, which
were really the cause of his death. Then we had another white woman, aged forty-six, and a white man
of twenty-eight. He was the last member of the group
to be treated or hospitalized, and he brought the total
up to twelve. An interesting group in age, color, and
sex. None of the other frequenters of Dalton's place
was hospitalized. I didn't see or talk to any of them,
but a couple of residents on my service got interested
in the outbreak, too, and they checked them out. They
all said they were or had been sick, but not sick
enough to seek treatment. So the total for the outbreak remained at twelve confirmed. Eleven of them
had serologic evidence of *C. burnetii* infection. The
twelfth, Raymond Kelly, the man who died, showed
evidence of infection at autopsy. Six of the twelve—
all male and all black—were seriously ill. One of the
women was moderately ill, and three women and the

61

one white man were only mildly infected. All of them, apart from Kelly, responded well to tetracycline and fully recovered.

"The incubation period in Q fever seems to range from fourteen to thirty-nine days. That's the interval between infection and the onset of illness. The average is around three weeks. What we wanted to know now was when those twelve people got sick. That would enable us to figure back and reach an approximate time of exposure to whatever was the source of infection. Then we could begin looking for the source. My residents and I started in on that line of questioning. Thomas Dalton, the owner of the Munich Street place, turned out to be the index case. That is, he was the first of the twelve to get sick. His onset was March fifth. The next victim, William Evans, took sick on March seventh. Andrews, the first patient I saw, took sick on March eighth. There were two onsets on the ninth, three on the tenth, two—including the fatal case—on the fourteenth, one the next day, and the last, the one white man, on the sixteenth. As a general rule, the more serious the infection, the shorter the incubation period. The five most serious cases had onsets within a period of only four days. The fatal case had a late onset, but he didn't figure in our calculations. We estimated that the time of exposure was probably in mid-February. We—the residents—went back to the patients again. They checked on the usual sources of infection. None of the eleven had any history of exposure to cattle, sheep, or goats. These were city people. None of them worked in meatpacking or such. None of them drank unpasteurized milk. None of them had recently been outside Nova Scotia. These inquiries were simply a matter of routine. We didn't expect to get any positive answers. We knew that the source of infection had to be the one place all the patients had in common—the poker room on Munich Street. I hadn't at this point seen or talked to Tom Dalton. I decided the time was now. He had left the hospital, and I reached him by telephone at his home. He was an easy, cheerful-sounding man. I said I had a couple of questions, and he said go ahead. Our conversation went something like this:

" 'Do you happen to have a cat?'

" 'Yes.'

" 'Is it a female?'

" 'Yes.'

" 'Did it recently have kittens?'

" 'Yes. There were three in the litter, but one was born dead.'

" 'When was that?'

" 'I think it was about February fourteenth.'

" 'Where did it happen?'

" 'She lives in the poker room. That's where she littered.'

" 'Was there a game going on that day?'

" 'There's always a game going on.'

"So I thanked him and hung up."

Dr. Marrie sat back in his chair and smiled. "Now," he said. "Why did I ask those questions? The answer is that I knew the answers, or I was pretty sure I did. And how did that happen? Because I had been there before. The textbook understanding of Q fever has never given cats a role in the epidemiology of the disease. That assumption was challenged here in Nova

Scotia a few years ago by a physician named Tom Ko-satsky. In the course of investigating a 1982 outbreak of thirteen cases of Q fever in a little fishing village down the coast, near Shelburne, Kosatsky was able to implicate a family cat—a cat that had recently given birth to kittens in the entryway of a house visited on that day or the next by all the victims. Kosatsky had, of course, first eliminated all the usual suspects. He reported his findings in a classic paper published in *The Lancet* in 1984. I've had similar experiences of my own. My first encounter was in 1985, in a village up in northern Nova Scotia, on Cape Breton Island. There were thirty-three cases, confirmed or probable, of Q fever, all of whom lived or worked in a group of ad-jacent buildings—three stores, a restaurant, and a taxi stand, all with apartments above. The epidemiology was much like that in the Kosatsky outbreak, but there was an interesting difference. One of the families in one of the apartments had a cat, and the cat had re-cently had kittens—all of them, as it happened, still-born. The interesting thing was this: all the victims had had contact with the cat, but they hadn't gone to the cat—the cat had gone to them. The cat was in the habit of roaming around the little community, and for three weeks before she gave birth she was bleeding from the vagina. Another experience of mine was a cat-related outbreak of Q fever in a small town over on the Bay of Fundy. The setting was a truck-repair plant that employed thirty-two men and women. Six-teen of them came down with Q fever. Several had to be hospitalized at our center here in Halifax. Their only common point of contact was the plant. The plant occupied a two-story building and some one-story annexes. The repair shop was on the ground floor, and the second floor was divided into an office and a parts department. There was no possible source of infection at the plant. No animals of any kind—not even a cat. But, it finally turned out, there *was* a cat involved. A man who worked in the parts department had one at home. His cat had recently had kittens. We learned that the mother refused to let her kittens nurse. The owner decided to take her place. Every morning, before going off to work he fed the kittens with an eyedropper. Well, there was the source of the outbreak. The kittens' basket was contaminated during the birthing, and that contamination was picked up and absorbed by the man's work clothes. The aerosols generated from his clothing infected him and those of his fellow-workers who had any close contact with him."

*Cherchez le chat.* "I see what you mean," I said. "And all those cases here in Halifax turned out to have been in the poker room on the day the cat was having her kittens?"

"That's right," Dr. Marrie said. "They were playing or waiting to play or just hanging around watching and drinking beer during most of that day. It was a small room, too—no more than fifteen feet square. And I don't suppose there was much ventilation—this was mid-February. The people who said they had some vague symptoms of illness probably just came and went. There was no question about the cat's being the source of the outbreak. We had a hysterectomy performed on her, and laboratory examination of the uterus demonstrated the presence of *C. burnetii*. I might add that the stillborn kitten was a significant factor in the outbreak. There is good evidence that exposure to a stillborn kitten tends to increase the risk of infection."

I nodded. That seemed to be that. But no—there was something that bothered me. I wondered how the *cat* had got infected.

"That bothered us, too," Dr. Marrie said. "This outbreak was different from the others. They were all in small communities near farms and open country. Cats roam. But Halifax is a city with a population of a hundred and twenty-five thousand or more, and Munich Street is near the center of town. All we have is a reasonable hypothesis. The Dalton cat had no possible contact with farm animals. But cats are mousers, and there are mice just about everywhere. Mice are not notorious carriers of disease vectors, like rats, but they can be a reservoir. They can harbor infected ticks and mites and such. That was established back in 1946, in a big outbreak of rickettsial pox down in New York City. We think the cat caught an infected mouse."

[*1989*]

# A Good, Safe Tan

D r. Richard Stein, an associate professor of medicine in the Department of Hematology at the Vanderbilt University School of Medicine, in Nashville, came back to his office from rounds one May morning in 1989 and found on his desk a memorandum from his secretary to telephone a Dr. Frank Lincoln (as I'll call him), in Denver. Dr. Lincoln was not known to Dr. Stein, but Vanderbilt's Department of Hematology is a distinguished one, and he was accustomed to such calls. He punched out the number, and Dr. Lincoln came on the line. He thanked Dr. Stein for returning his call. He had, he said, a young woman patient with aplastic anemia, and it was his understanding that Vanderbilt had access to rabbit antilymphocyte serum. If so, he would like to refer her to Vanderbilt for treatment. Dr. Stein said yes, it was true that Vanderbilt had access to rabbit antilymphocyte serum. The serum was, in fact, made in Nashville. He said he would be happy to receive the young woman. But how, he added, was she responding to blood transfusions? Aplastic anemia, the rarest and by far the most ferocious of the several anemias, is the devastating consequence of an assault—by the scorch of radiation, by the direct attack of some toxic substance, by certain viruses, or perhaps by still unidentified substances—on the bone marrow and its ability to manufacture erythrocytes, or red blood cells. Transfusion of red blood cells and platelets will restore, at least temporarily, the body's essential supply of blood. Antilymphocyte serum may, in time, and in some cases, if the bone-marrow destruction has not been overwhelming, have the power to regenerate the production of stem, or progenitor, cells. Well, Dr. Lincoln said, that was just the problem. The patient steadfastly refused transfusions. The acceptance of another person's blood was abhorrent to her. It was a matter of religious faith. She was a Jehovah's Witness.

"That gave me pause," Dr. Stein told me in a conversation we had not long ago in his office. He is in his early forties, dark-haired and balding, quick to laugh, quick to frown, with a gesture for every mood, every remark or observation. He is a graduate of Harvard College and Harvard Medical School, a member of Phi Beta Kappa, and, to judge from his office, whose walls are decorated with mounted baseball cards, Chicago Cubs pennants, and a clock in the shape of the Cubs' logo, a baseball fan of some stature.

"It wasn't exactly her religion that made me hesitate. I've treated a number of Jehovah's Witnesses with blood diseases, and I respect their beliefs. I mean, I accept them. But I like to get one thing straight from the start. Just how steadfast is their refusal to accept a blood transfusion? Is the conviction their own? Or is it influenced by parents or spouse? I can deal with disappointment or failure. I won't put up with equivocation. So I told Dr. Lincoln frankly that I would accept his patient only if she or her parents or her husband, if she had one, called me. I wanted a frank discussion of the transfusion question. Dr. Lincoln assured me that that could be arranged. His patient— let's call her Penny Thompson—was just twenty; she was unmarried and lived with her parents in a small town in the Midwest. A local doctor had referred her to Dr. Lincoln. He said he would call there and arrange for one of her parents to call me. An hour or two later, I got a call from Mrs. Thompson. She assured me that she and her husband and Penny were in complete agreement, and that Penny would rather die than accept any transfusions. I wondered if that was just a figure of speech. Because if Penny wasn't transfused it was only too likely that she *would* die. Mrs. Thompson said that the family stood firm. They were prepared to face that possibility. I had to believe her. I said all right, I'd accept Penny as a patient and we would do the best we could for her. There was perhaps an outside chance that antilymphocyte therapy might regenerate her bone marrow.

"Penny arrived here on June fifth and was admitted to my service. I saw her for the first time, I think, on the following day. I had her history in hand. She had been worked up on admission by one of my residents. Here was her medical history: She had been ill with malaise, headache, increasing fatigue, easy bruising, and some weight loss over the past four months. The diagnosis of aplastic anemia had been confirmed by a bone-marrow biopsy and aspiration. She was negative for any past illnesses that might have contributed to her anemia, such as hepatitis B. She had taken no medications, she was not aware of any exposure to chemicals or pesticides. She didn't smoke or drink. She had never been pregnant. She lived at home and was a student at a secretarial school. Her background was remarkable in only one respect. She said that several weeks before she became sick she had visited a local tanning salon. She had been given a supply of tablets that, she was told, would produce a good tan and a safe one. That impressed her. She had a very fair complexion, and sunbathing gave her only sunburn. The idea of a good tan was very attractive, and the assurance that it was safe was also appealing. The people at the tanning salon explained the process. The tablets contained a vegetable dye known as canthaxanthin. When ingested, the tablets produced an attractive tan by depositing the color beneath the skin. There was no ultraviolet-ray involvement. No possibility of burning or, worse, skin cancer. I had no knowledge of canthaxanthin. Frankly, I had never heard of it. Was that a possible source of her trouble? But aplastic anemia is aplastic anemia, whatever the cause. My only concern was to try to keep her alive. And that looked very hard to do. Her hematocrit was really disheartening. A hematocrit is a measure of red-blood-cell volume. The normal range for women is

from thirty-seven to forty-seven percent. Her hematocrit at admission was just thirteen."

Dr. Stein continued, "My first glimpse of Penny was
a shock. In spite of her history, I wasn't prepared for
what I saw. She was sitting propped up in bed, and
what I could see of her, of her skin—her arms and
hands and face—was an awful shade of orange. So
that was her wonderful tanning-parlor tan! It was in-
human. Frankly, she was a sight. It was so pathetic.
She had pale red hair of the kind that goes with the
fairest, almost translucent complexion, and big, pale
blue eyes, framed in that awful shade of orange. And
thin! She couldn't have weighed a hundred pounds. I
knew she was twenty years old. But she looked about
fourteen. Was she pretty? Attractive? Not really. She
was, I guess you could say, sweet. Appealing. Like a
waif. I smiled and said hello and introduced myself. I
told her I was her attending physician. But all the time
I was thinking of what was probably going to happen
to her, and knowing there was so little I could do
about it. It was terrible.

"I sat down and began to get acquainted. She said
she was comfortable. She was not in any kind of pain.
She was just a little weak. She had been driven down
to Nashville and had felt no particular strain during
the trip. She had walked into the hospital. She said
she understood the nature of her trouble and its im-
plications, and she knew the established treatment
was blood transfusion. And no, she would never sub-
mit to such a thing. Her mind was still firm on that.
Yes, she realized that she was in real danger. I had
been prepared for what she was saying, but it was aw-

ful to hear her saying it. I mean, she seemed such a child. We talked about what we could do for her—about the antilymphocyte-serum therapy. I told her that the serum alone was unlikely to help her. We could only hope. As I said, I've had Jehovah's Witnesses as patients before, and I've known them to change their minds at the last moment. The urge to live is pretty strong. Especially in someone as young as she. She had a very small, very quiet voice. But she was absolutely firm in her resolve.

"That was only the first of a number of frustrating talks. We treated her as best we could, with the rabbit serum and a number of supportive measures. But, of course, it wasn't enough. She began to feel less comfortable. She developed a hot feeling in her back, and what she described as a burning sensation in her stomach. She complained—no, she never complained. She *reported* a rapid heartbeat and shortness of breath. I saw her and talked with her every day. After a few days, she could still walk but only with some support. Then she was too weak to walk even with help. So now she was totally bedridden. We treated her symptoms as best we could. I still had some hope. I talked blood transfusions every day. I've never been so frustrated in my life. I teach in the medical ethics program here. Our position is always that the patient's beliefs must be honored. But it was so difficult. *My* convictions were being tested as well as hers. My house staff presented another problem. There was a chance of saving her life. Not much of one, but still a chance. And they were reluctant, to put it mildly, to stand idly by. All doctors lose patients because the best they can do just isn't enough. But here we were simply blocked by Penny's absolute, unwavering determination. It was an experience I can never forget. I told her flatly—I said, 'Penny, you may very well die.' She said, 'If that's the way it is, that's the way it is.' And that's the way it was. Her hematocrit continued to fall. It finally dropped to eight percent. I had to tell her the inescapable truth. She *was* dying. She had only a very few more days to live. I remember her lying there, too weak now even to raise her head off the pillow. She said, 'Well, then—I want to go home. I want to die at home.' And so it was arranged. She was discharged on June twenty-eighth. She had been with us just over three weeks. Some friends came down in a van and picked her up and drove her home. It must have been a pretty grim journey.

"A couple of weeks went by. Then one day I got a call from Mrs. Thompson. It was something about— I've forgotten what. Maybe about a bill. Anyway, I asked her about Penny. She said Penny was dead. She had died only an hour or two after she got home."

On June 7, two days after Penny Thompson's arrival at Vanderbilt University Medical Center, a copy of her admittance chart was delivered to the Division of Clinical Pharmacology and routed to the office of a physician and assistant professor of medicine and clinical pharmacology there named Renata Bluhm. That was standard procedure. The admittance charts of all patients at Vanderbilt are reviewed by a drug-surveillance clerk for any reference to unusual drugs, and such findings are then dispatched to Clinical Pharmacology to be studied and evaluated for possible association with the patient's complaint. I went around to Dr. Bluhm's office in the course of my stay in Nashville and talked with her about her involvement in the case of Penny Thompson. I found Dr. Bluhm—an attractive woman of about forty, with soft brown hair and a gentle voice, a native of Germany and a graduate of the University of Illinois in both medicine and pharmacology—in a tiny room given over almost entirely to bookcases and filing cabinets.

I took a sort of seat on a chest, and asked Dr. Bluhm about canthaxanthin. She smiled a little smile. She said that it now seemed so hard to believe she had once known nothing whatever about it. Like Dr. Stein, she had never even heard of it until she read Penny Thompson's chart. She had not, however, shared his indifference to it. She was instantly interested, instantly fascinated. There was nothing she could do to help Penny Thompson. The chart made it clear that Penny was dying. It was also clear to her that Penny was suffering from aplastic anemia, a condition whose usual causes are pretty well known. But there were none of those in Penny's history. No drugs, no immunological problems. But something had caused her illness and something had caused her color. Something was still causing it; she was still orange. Everything centered on canthaxanthin. It was the only unknown. Dr. Bluhm told me that she had started in that afternoon on a search of the literature. She turned first, as a matter of course, to *The Pharmacological Basis of Therapeutics*, by Louis S. Goodman and Alfred Gilman, the standard work in the field. There was no reference to canthaxanthin. That meant that it was probably not a prescription drug, or even an over-the-counter drug in good repute. It was

74

not an aspirin or an Ex-Lax or a Maalox. That also meant that she would need to dig deeper and into a different literature.

Dr. Bluhm dug deep for another hour or two. She came up with a reference that led her to the February 1987 issue of a periodical called *Drug Intelligence & Clinical Pharmacy*, to an article headed "Drug Information Analysis Service," and to a section subtitled "Indications and Safety of Canthaxanthine." That put her feet firmly on the ground. Canthaxanthin, she learned, is a member of the carotenoid family of compounds. Its chemical designation is beta-carotene-4,4'-dione. Carotene is a widely distributed coloring agent. It is what gives such vegetables as carrots, sweet potatoes, and squash their orange color. It is also found in the wild in mushrooms, in shellfish, in birds, in algae. The canthaxanthin in commercial use is produced synthetically, and is recognized by the United States Food and Drug Administration as an acceptable food-coloring agent. It is a common, if rarely proclaimed, source of the buttery color of much butter, and it is widely used to enrich the color of cheese, to burnish the natural brown of ketchup to the expected red, to enhance the eye appeal of pizzas and of spaghetti and barbecue sauces. Chicken growers frequently add canthaxanthin to chicken feed to give the skin of their birds the golden yellow color that we are taught to associate with fresh and healthy birds. The golden yolks of eggs that consumers have learned to prefer are often achieved by a henhouse diet of canthaxanthin. The use of canthaxanthin as a food additive is strictly controlled. The FDA estimates that the daily intake of canthaxanthin of the average person never exceeds 5.6 milligrams in a normal diet. The use of canthaxanthin for any other purpose is illegal. Indeed, Dr. Bluhm found a study published in *Clinical Toxicology of Commercial Products, Acute Poisoning*, in 1976, that gave it a rating of "moderately toxic." She went on to tell me that canthaxanthin shares with the other carotenoids little more than its pigmentary powers. These powers, however, are considerable. It is fat-soluble, and is absorbed into fatty tissue throughout the body. Its accumulation is not confined to the subcutaneous tissue, where it so bizarrely colored Penny Thompson's skin. It colors the liver, the lungs, the bone marrow, the blood, even the stool. There is evidence that it can also color the body of a fetus. Most carotenoids are precursors of vitamin A. They are converted into vitamin A in the course of their metabolization. Canthaxanthin is unpleasantly different. It cannot be converted into vitamin A. Nor is it easily oxidized and thus eliminated from the body. That essential process (everything that the body takes in must be either utilized or discarded) may take many days or weeks, or even months. This leisurely departure was clearly demonstrated by the persistence of Penny Thompson's peculiar color until she died. It occurred to me as Dr. Bluhm and I talked that canthaxanthin, in its unnaturally procrastinated withdrawal, much resembles the notoriously toxic sojourn of methyl alcohol in the bodies of those foolish enough or desperate enough to drink it.

And yet. Dr. Bluhm opened a folder on her desk and took out a full-color advertisement on slick paper from a Sunday newspaper supplement. It was a full page, a page about the size of a news magazine. It was headed TAN BEAUTIFULLY SUN-FREE. Below that was "Have the rich dark year-round tan you want without aging your skin." Below that were two photographs of young women in bikini bathing suits. One of them was pale skinned and solidly built, with long, lank hair and a glum expression, posed as for a police lineup. The other, with a lovely smiling face framed in a luxuriant mane of hair, was enticingly posed, and her figure, slim and shapely, was tanned a luscious brown. Her glorious tan, it was pointed out, was the creation of something called Darker Tan. "Millions," I read, "have gained a beautiful golden-bronze deep tan by simply taking 3 or 4 tablets of the Darker Tan formula (31 mg of Canthaxanthin per tablet) per day until they are as dark as they want to be. . . . Darker Tan's active ingredient, Canthaxanthin, is organic, natural, and harmless. . . . The U.S. Food and Drug Administration approved Canthaxanthin long ago and still does as a food coloring agent in many of the foods you eat today." I read on: "The Sun's Rays Cause Skin Cancer." There was an announcement: "Introductory Discount 50% off. . . . 101 tablets . . . $18.90." Readers were directed to an address in Las Vegas. Darker Tan ended its exhortation with a wink: "Warning: Both men and women have reported cases of too much attention from the opposite sex after taking Darker Tan causing jealousy of spouses or dates."

Dr. Bluhm took back Darker Tan and gave me another, very similar advertisement. It offered, from an address in Columbus, Ohio, a canthaxanthin tanning tablet called BronzGlo. It, too, featured two young women in bikinis: "What a difference a tan makes!" The text might well have been written by the same hand that celebrated Darker Tan: "The sun's UV radiation causes skin damage and skin cancer. . . . Completely Safe: Canthaxanthin, the active ingredient in BronzGlo, is a totally harmless, natural, organic substance . . . is included as a food coloring agent in many of the foods you eat and is approved for that purpose by the U.S. Food and Drug Administration." The recommended dose for those seeking a tan was "3 or 4 tablets . . . (30 mg of Canthaxanthin per tablet) per day until they are as dark as they wish to be." The price ("Introductory 40% Discount") for a hundred tablets was $18.95. There was no warning. There was, instead, a warm assurance: "Your rich tan will give you a glow of health, energy and attractiveness that will make you the envy of all of your friends."

Dr. Bluhm dipped once more into her folder. I exchanged BronzGlo for an advertisement for The Tan Line, doing business at an 800 number in Costa Mesa, California. The Tan Line was all tough-minded business. No color, no photographs, just "Canthaxanthin Information. This information is VERY important. Please read it!" I skimmed the information. "The tablets MUST be taken with meals and at different meals throughout the day." There was a somewhat Jesuitical warning: "Excessive vitamin A can cause vitamin A toxicity which could lead to liver damage. . . . Canthaxanthin is not pro–vitamin A." It ended on another warning: "Compliance with any law is the purchaser's responsibility." Caveat emptor!

And there was more to come. The advertisements for Darker Tan, BronzGlo, and The Tan Line had appeared in newspaper supplements with a general, unpretentious readership. But Dr. Bluhm's research had turned up an exception—a reference to an advertisement in a magazine of impeccable upmarket appeal. The advertisement acclaimed a fourth canthaxanthin product, this one called The Tanning Pill, and it had run in the November 1984 issue of *Harper's Bazaar*.

Dr. Bluhm closed her advertising folder. "Did you notice?" she said. "There's something interesting about canthaxanthin that none of these people ever mention. They all emphasize that exposure to the sun can cause skin aging, and even cancer. And that's perfectly true. But what they don't say is that a canthaxanthin tan offers no more protection against the sun's ultraviolet radiation than no tan at all. One could have a beautiful canthaxanthin tan and still get badly sunburned."

Dr. Bluhm's immediate search of the literature satisfied her immediate curiosity about the nature of canthaxanthin, but her interest in the matter remained. Indeed, the more she learned the more her interest grew. Everything about it and its outlawed manipulation excited her. She found herself enjoyably charged with a sense of mission.

Her first thrust in that direction was a report of the case of Penny Thompson—which she wrote in collaboration with Dr. Stein and two other colleagues, Dr. Robert Branch and Dr. Philip Johnston—to the *Journal of the American Medical Association*. It was published in the issue of September 5, 1990. The report, as required, was scrupulously clinical, but it concluded with a word of comment and concern: "Although definitive evidence is lacking for the role of canthaxanthin as a cause of the patient's aplastic anemia, the history of onset of symptoms several weeks after the use of canthaxanthin without any other apparent cause suggests the association of this toxic effect with canthaxanthin. . . . Since no studies have been carried out in humans to evaluate the safety of canthaxanthin as an oral tanning agent, advertising statements that the drug is harmless have no foundation. More careful investigation . . . is needed."

The publication of "Aplastic Anemia Associated with Canthaxanthin Ingested for 'Tanning' Purposes," as the article by Dr. Bluhm and her associates was titled, attracted wide and serious attention. Responses to it ranged from an anecdotal note from a physician in Florida to a "Talk Paper," or position report, headed "Update on Tanning Pills," from the Food and Drug Administration. The physician introduced himself as an avocational canary breeder. He wrote that he had conceived the idea of feeding canthaxanthin to his birds in the hope of producing a brilliantly red-feathered variant strain. He said that he had had one or two successes, but that several of his canaries that were fed canthaxanthin had died of a wasting blood disease. The *JAMA* report, he wrote to Dr. Bluhm, would seem to have explained those deaths. The FDA "Talk Paper" was dated October 1 and began, "F.D.A. continues to warn consumers that canthaxanthin— the major ingredient in tanning pills—has not been approved by the agency as safe for this or any other cosmetic use. Such products are illegal. The agency advises that statements claiming the ingredient has been approved are misleading. The ingredient has been approved, at very low levels, for coloring some foods and drugs, but not, at any level, for tanning pur-

poses. . . . The 1960 Color Additive Amendments require manufacturers to petition F.D.A. to approve
each proposed use of a color additive. Legally, all
color additives are considered unsafe unless data
prove otherwise." The case reported by Dr. Bluhm and
her associates was not the first canthaxanthin tanning-
pill complaint to come to the FDA's attention. A young
woman became seriously ill after taking tablets every
day for two months. Her illness was diagnosed as
drug-induced hepatitis. A man developed welts and severe itching after taking only eight tablets. Penny
Thompson's aplastic anemia was merely the first such
case on record.

"I went down to one of our health-food stores the
other day," Dr. Bluhm told me. "Canthaxanthin had
made me very curious about that sort of place, the sort
of place where you can buy tanning tablets. I wanted
to see their display of drugs. There are, of course,
drugs and drugs. The drugs that most of us are familiar with are what I call ethical drugs. I use that term
to describe both prescription drugs and over-the-
counter drugs. They differ, generally speaking, in only
one respect: prescription drugs require the authori-
zation of a physician. But both are equally safe, both
have been tested and approved by the FDA for certain
specified uses. Then, there are what I call nonethical
drugs. Some of these, like canthaxanthin, have been
declared illegal for any but a designated use. But most
of them are simply nonlegal. There are probably many
hundreds of them, but they don't exist in any standard
index or pharmacopoeia. Their effectiveness or inef-
fectiveness—even their toxicity—has never been sci-

entifically established. They form a sort of gray area that has always interested me, but canthaxanthin made me really concerned. The truly illicit drugs don't interest me in the same way. Heroin, cocaine, LSD, all those. The people who take those drugs know what they're doing. And they take them not only for an expected result. Their adrenaline is turned on by more than the drug itself. They know there is a risk—anything might happen—and that risk is part of the experience. There is an excitement in a jump into the unknown. But, as I say, this is not my main concern. My main concern is for the unsophisticated, the innocent, the ignorant and gullible people who go to the health stores in the hope of improving their health.

"The store I went to was doing a good business. I suppose they all do. I browsed along the shelves. The drugs and food supplements and tonics all had labels and names and usually some suggestion of purpose. But that was it. There was no real information. Canthaxanthin tanning pills were on display, and a reporter I know on one of the local papers later told me there were also a number of tanning parlors around town where they were featured. Well, I asked the clerk about some of the things they stocked. He shook his head. He didn't know. He said he just worked there. I wish I had taken some good notes. But I have an advertisement from some magazine or paper that tells the same story."

Dr. Bluhm shuffled through her folder and pulled out still another clipping. She spread it out on her desk. It was a full-page listing of counterculture pharmaceuticals that could be obtained from a nameless 800 number. It told a story, all right. And a sad one.

The page was headed JBN KEEPS YOU AND YOUR WALLET IN SHAPE. The first item on the list was "Aminobolic P.M., 14 Day, $9.99." Another was "Good Life Mega Pack," at the same price. There was a "Victory Coenzyme Q-10," priced at $17.39 for "100 caps." There was "Life Essence Amino Caps," for only a few cents more. There was "Victory Smilax & Siberian Ginseng, 180 caps, $7.19." There was "Victory Ferulic Acid, 60 caps, $12.59." And a good dozen more. Bodybuilders all.

"You will notice that none of them are described," Dr. Bluhm said. "There are no claims, except by implication. The names sound beneficial, and scientifically impressive. People have heard of the amino acids. They may not know precisely that they are essential components of the protein molecule, but they know they're supposed to be good for you. So 'Aminobolic P.M.' and 'Life Essence Amino' sound good. Ferulic acid is better known as asafetida, which has a strong odor and a strong flavor. I understand that it is a zesty ingredient of Worcestershire sauce. But it is chiefly a famous folk remedy—for asthma, convulsions, insanity, croup, cancer, and all the rest. Smilax is a plant of the family that includes catbrier. And ginseng is a traditional Asian aphrodisiac. A coenzyme is a molecule necessary to enzyme function, and an enzyme is, of course, a protein. Nutrition again. So you pay your money—or, rather, as it says here, 'MasterCard, Visa, Discover accepted'—and who knows just what you get? Is it toxic? Or is it harmless, just a waste of your money?"

I thought of the shrug of warning in the ad for The Tan Line. Only, here there wasn't even that. This time, I said aloud what I'd thought: "Caveat emptor."

"Yes," Dr. Bluhm said. "There is a serious problem here. I think it is a problem of both information and control. The amino acids are a good case in point. It's the same problem we have with canthaxanthin. For many years, the FDA classified amino acids as 'generally recognized as safe.' Then, around 1970, it was suggested, on the basis of animal experiments, that large quantities of individual amino acids posed a potential health risk, and the FDA removed them from the 'safe' list. I'm sure you remember the L-tryptophan tragedy of a couple of years ago. Twenty-eight people died, mainly in the Southwest, and fifteen hundred became seriously ill. L-tryptophan is an amino acid sold in the health stores as a 'food supplement.' It had been banned since 1972, except for certain regulated uses, but it remained on sale in all the stores. The L-tryptophan that caused the disaster was found to have been contaminated. But, contaminated or not, L-tryptophan should not have been on sale. Just like canthaxanthin.

"Now, here's the problem. The FDA, through its public-relations activities, has impressed on the American public that its reviews of drugs are stringent, lengthy, and comprehensive. So the public naturally assumes that the drugs it sees advertised and on sale are safe and effective. That, unfortunately, is not the case. The FDA drug reviews are stringent and lengthy. They are not comprehensive. The trouble is that the federal regulatory agencies do not as a rule initiate the drug reviews. The usual procedure is for the manufacturer to invite such a review. The makers of the drugs I call ethical all prudently follow that procedure. But if a drug is not offered for review it is not as a matter of course reviewed, and it may then simply be placed on sale. Canthaxanthin has been cited by the FDA as unsafe except for food coloring. The amino acids have also been banned, except for certain regulated uses. And yet they remain on sale. But, more than that, there are probably hundreds of other non-ethical drugs on sale and unknown to the FDA. I think the review system should itself be reviewed. What is needed is an open information resource that would make available to the consumer essential information about those hundreds of nonethical drugs—the chemical constituents, the physiological effects, the toxicity."

The telephone rang. Dr. Bluhm answered it, and talked softly for a moment or two, in her light, gentle voice. She hung up, and sat for another moment or two. "Where was I?" she said. "Well—no matter. It's not enough to say that Penny Thompson died because she refused blood transfusions. The fact is that she did have aplastic anemia, an extremely serious disease. It is not enough to say that she is the only known case of aplastic anemia associated with canthaxanthin tanning pills. In her case, the bone marrow was practically destroyed. But it is quite possible that many men and women taking canthaxanthin tanning pills are suffering some subclinical bone-marrow suppression. I think of the history of the antibiotic chloramphenicol. It was one of the first broad-spectrum drugs. It was hailed as a true miracle drug. It was prescribed to thousands of patients, with wonderful results. Then a patient died. Of—as it happened—aplastic anemia. A thorough review established that it was wonderfully effective but could also be extremely toxic in its side effects. Chloramphenicol is still prescribed, but only as a last resort, when the need justifies the risk. The risk in canthaxanthin may be very slight. But does a cosmetic justify any risk?"

[*1991*]

# Overdoing It

The greatest evil is physical pain.
—St. Augustine

In the late summer of 1986, when her peculiar pains began and insidiously worsened, Mary-Margaret Carden (Mrs. Gerald Harris) was, and had been for some years, the organist at the First United Methodist Church in Fort Smith, Arkansas, the largest church (with a congregation of more than three thousand) in town. She was also an active partner in the Carden-Harris Azalea Nursery, in the hamlet of Branch, a few miles west of Fort Smith, where she and her husband make their home. She was then thirty-six years old, and her past medical history, in the backhanded language of medicine, was "unremarkable."

"I had no medical history," Miss Carden says. "I had always been healthy. I'd always worked hard, and I loved my work—both jobs. Nursery work is hard work, but it's seasonal. The organ was all year long, and every day of the week. It wasn't only the Sunday services. All musicians have to practice regularly, and I was practicing two hours every day on my own. Then there were the church rehearsals. Two nonstop hours. Then there were the weddings. In a church the size of ours, there are a whole lot of weddings. Weddings are killers. I mean, prenuptial music is much nicer than just background music, but it's much more demanding. I knew I was probably overdoing it, but it's hard to change your habits. My first symptoms appeared around the end of August. I'd had a long weekend at the church. The first pain was in my right wrist. Every time I moved my hand or my fingers, it radiated up my arm. And there was a strange feeling in my ring and little fingers. It was a dead feeling. I should say that I'm left-handed. That may explain why the pain started in my right hand, my weaker hand. My first thought was that it had something to do with the way I'm made. I have rather large hands for a woman. I can stretch an octave and two notes more. But my wrists are small. I thought maybe it was just that they were weak. This went on for a time. Then the church decided to replace the organ, to install a new one. During the change-over, I had to use a piano. Many people think that a piano and an organ are much the same. Actually, about the only thing that they have in common is the keyboard. The organ is much less physically demanding. The dynamics are controlled by devices called stops and pedals, not by finger pressure. The piano is, in that respect, a percussion instrument. I think those days at the piano are what did it. The pain got really worse. I knew there was something seriously wrong. So I called the doctor, an internist, and made an appointment.

"The doctor was sympathetic. He agreed with me that I had probably been overdoing it. He put me in an arm splint—my right arm—to be worn at night to minimize movement. He wrote a prescription for an anti-inflammatory drug. He advised me to cut back on my playing. I followed his advice for several weeks. I wore the splint, I took the drug, I tried to reduce my playing time. None of it helped, and I finally lost confidence. I saw an orthopedist. He X-rayed my arms— both arms—and the results, he said, were normal. He gave me a prescription for an anti-inflammatory drug. His drug was no more effective than the first one. I was still in pain. I went to another doctor, another orthopedist. He also X-rayed my hands and arms. He said he thought I had a vascular problem, and prescribed aspirin, eight a day for a month. All the aspirin did was to eat up my stomach and make me feel I was going deaf. I was still in pain, worse than ever. I managed to get through the Christmas season. My symptoms at this point were continued numbness in both hands, ring fingers and little fingers. I had pain in both hands now, but the right wrist was the worst. I seemed to be losing the muscles in both hands. And both hands would get cold and white. It was as though there was something interfering with the blood supply. But the worst symptom was a loss of control of my hands. I would be playing—the new organ or, sometimes, the piano—and there would be almost a short circuit between my brain and my hands. My fingers felt as though they had not had an organ or a piano lesson since age eight. I couldn't play even the most familiar hymns without making mistakes."

Miss Carden gave up her job at the church just after Christmas. The organ had become an instrument not only of pain but also of embarrassment. She did nothing in the first weeks of 1987. The nursery was in its dormant season. She rested and hoped for the best— a recovery, a remission. But the pain that came alive at almost any sustained use of her hands continued, along with the lack of feeling and the awkward finger articulation. In late January, she sought out another doctor, an internist. He felt she needed more specialized observation than he could provide, and referred her to a neurologist for clinical evaluation. The neurologist's examination included an electromyographic procedure. An EMG, as it is briskly called, records and studies the electrical properties of skeletal muscle to determine abnormal function. The findings were largely inconclusive. They showed only some indistinct impairment of the ulnar nerve. The ulnar nerve is one of the three nerves that energize the forearm, and through its intricacy of branches it mediates the function of the hand and fingers. Most people, sooner or later, become acutely aware of the ulnar nerve and its exquisite sensitivity; but they seldom know it by that name. They know it as the "funny bone" or "crazy bone." He gave her the inevitable prescription for an anti-inflammatory drug, and asked her to return in March. Miss Carden went home and waited. The March consultation included a thorough neurological examination, the results of which were essentially normal. The neurologist noted his impression on her chart: "Right upper-extremity ulnar-nerve neuralgia, with evidence of bilateral ulnar neuropathy of a mild degree. . . . I suspect it is occupation-related and is most likely due to inflammation and injury at the level of the wrist." He gave her a prescription for Motrin (a painkiller and an anti-inflammatory drug) and an appointment in April. At her April consultation, Miss Carden reported that there had been no improvement, and that she had received no relief from Motrin. The neurologist responded with a notation on her chart: "I would like to see if there is any possible joint-related cause . . . that may be contributing to her symptoms in view of her occupation." He arranged an appointment for her with a rheumatologist.

The rheumatologist saw her the following week. That was the last week in April. His examination was fully comprehensive. It embraced a review of systems, a standard physical examination, and a detailed scrutiny of her bones, joints, and extremities. The results were all essentially unremarkable. Supplementary laboratory studies were negative for any evidence of arthritis. The doctor noted in passing, and without comment, that Miss Carden habitually smoked one package of cigarettes a day, and that she was allergic to penicillin. His concluding assessment, as noted on her now voluminous chart, was "no obvious signs of connective-tissue disease." But experience has taught most physicians to leave a door of some kind ajar. And he added, "Must consider also a regional musculo-skeletal disorder." He recommended to his neurological colleague that the patient be put on a regimen of analgesic and anti-inflammatory druggery, and that an antidepressant be considered.

Miss Carden returned once again to her puzzled neurologist. He suggested this time that a new EMG might throw a brighter light on the nature of her trouble. The test was performed, but, as before, the findings were uninstructive. The neurologist then proposed a consultation with a neurosurgeon. The surgeon, after another careful examination, informed her that any surgical intervention at this point would involve an unjustified risk. He said he would reconsider his position only if shown an unequivocally conclusive EMG report. There was no such EMG forthcoming. Summer arrived, and Miss Carden resumed her usual activities at the nursery. Or, rather, she made an attempt. Nursery work is not only heavy labor but also includes such finer operations as pruning and transplanting, which involve constant and repetitive use of the hands and fingers. Azalea growing is particularly demanding. Miss Carden made an effort to do what she had always done, and gave it up. In spite of all those months of drugs, the pain was still and always there. She could no longer do even her usual office work. Typing was as painful as pruning. So, it soon developed, was brushing her teeth and buttoning buttons and using a knife and fork. It is hard, however, to abandon hope, and in September she again appealed to her neurologist. He found no significant changes in her ulnar-nerve function. He perceived some slight improvement in neural transmission. His summary note on her chart was "Further clinical correlation is indicated." Hope still persisted. In November, she had what turned out to be a final consultation with her neurologist. It was much like all the others.

The neurologist's final entry on her chart read "Further clinical correlation is indicated."

"Well," Miss Carden says, "I finally gave up. After a year and a half of seeing doctors, taking drugs, and spending a fortune, I just gave up. I mean, what was the use? I resigned myself to living the way I was. Abandoning the organ was the hardest part. I was thirty-seven years old, and I had been playing for churches since I was sixteen. Still, looking back on all those doctors, I think I can kind of forgive them. They tried. In the beginning, I believed everything the doctors said. Then I began to realize that doctors aren't perfect, they can't know everything. But I have to say that during all those months I was angry and frustrated and depressed. Sometimes I wasn't even sure that I had a problem. Sooner or later, doubt does creep in. The things they told me! One of their ideas was that it was all a premenstrual syndrome. I began to feel that they were maybe a little skeptical of my whole complaint. Nobody actually suggested that I see a psychiatrist, but I got to the point where I almost expected it. I mean, I began to wonder about myself. I thought, Maybe I *am* a little nuts. I got so tired of their 'Take this medicine and come back in three months.' I think that toward the end all they really wanted was to get rid of me."

Miss Carden lived her life of retirement and resignation through the winter and spring of 1988. Then, around the end of May, she suddenly let herself hope once more. The March 28 issue of *Time* ran a story, under the department heading "Health & Fitness," about the health problems of performing artists. Among the several medical specialists mentioned was an associate professor of neurology at the University of Texas Medical School at Houston named Alan Lockwood, and the article carried a photograph of Dr. Lockwood with a woman seated at an organ. "I don't see *Time*," Miss Carden says, "but a friend of mine came across a copy of that issue somewhere— at the library, maybe, or in the dentist's office. Anyway, when she saw that photograph she thought of me. And gave me a call. She thought I might be interested. Interested! I got hold of a copy. That photograph! A woman organist. An organ. A doctor in a long white coat. Well, let's just say I was encouraged. I mean, here was a doctor who actually took an organist's problems seriously. But I was also half afraid. It was Gerald, my husband, who put in a call to Dr. Lockwood, and told him my story. That was on a Friday. Dr. Lockwood said, 'Well, why don't you bring her down on Monday.' "

Dr. Lockwood, a native of upstate New York and a graduate of the Cornell University Medical College, is a tall, lanky, blithely serious man in his late forties whose frosty workaday coat is usually enlivened by a striped shirt and a figured bow tie. His academic appointment at the University of Texas Medical School at Houston, demanding as it is, represents only one aspect of his life in medicine. He is also, and perhaps more conspicuously, the director of the Performing Artists' Clinic there. He was, in fact, its founder.

"I think the best way to explain the clinic is this," Dr. Lockwood told me. "I'm a frustrated musician. I've always loved music—classical music, choral music, opera. When I was still at Cornell, I was considered to have a promising tenor voice. I sang professionally with a group in New York until I had the misfortune of going out to Fire Island for a weekend and choking on a french fry. That took the promise out of my voice. But I have a teenage son who plays the cello, and has real professional talent. That gives me great pleasure. On the subject of family, I should say that I have a daughter who is developing into a linguist, and that appeals to my intellectual side. And my wife is a balance to my science. She's a psychologist. Well, Houston is a very musical city. We came here from the University of Miami in 1983, and one of the first things I interested myself in, outside of my work, was the Houston Symphony Orchestra. Pretty soon, I found myself on the board. One night I was talking to the personnel manager. He also plays the English horn. And he said something like, 'Here we are in the largest medical center in the country, but when one of our musicians has some medical problem, he has to travel up to Cleveland or Chicago.' I kept thinking about that. The idea intrigued me. I started reading in that direction. I wondered if I could manage that area of neuromuscular problems. My special interest at that time was the effect of liver disease on brain function. I began to study this new idea, and then the dean here offered to send me out to Aspen to sit in on a special program on the medical problems of musicians. In 1986, I decided I was ready. I announced my new specialty to the press office here, and hung out my shingle. So the Performing Artists' Clinic came into being. It has grown since then, and it is still growing. We have a staff that includes not only some colleagues of mine in neurology but also orthopedists and rheumatologists. And a lot of them are themselves musicians. So they have actually been there with the patient."

The medical problems of musicians that are directly related to their profession are many and often of great complexity. Those most frequently encountered at Dr. Lockwood's clinic include tendinitis, nerve-compression syndromes, motor-control problems, stress, and performance anxiety. With the possible exception of the last (whose roots are primarily emotional), these disabilities share the common denominator of pain. There are few pathological phenomena in medicine more easily understood than pain, and few more difficult to explain and define. This is, of course, because, whatever its source, pain is a wholly subjective experience, and the perception of its intensity tends to vary with the nature and the composure of the sufferer. Yet it is not the intensity of pain that is most painful. It is its duration. And the fear of what it might mean. A stubbed toe is more exquisitely painful than a sick headache, but since it is a sudden blaze, rather than a lingering smolder, it is far less uncomfortable. Still, for all the ambiguities of its constitution, pain is unequivocally a proclamation, a cry of warning. It is a symptom not to be ignored, and one of the stranger credulities of our time is the widespread contradiction of this fact.

"Nothing," Dr. Lockwood says, "is farther from the truth than the marathoner's maxim 'No pain, no gain.' Pain is not a badge of honor. It is a sign of tissue injury. The usual cause of pain among musicians is overdoing it: too much practice, too much playing. Some instruments are more demanding than others. They require more technical skill and more physical dexterity. There is an analogy in baseball. When a pitcher throws a fastball, it is a natural, overhand motion. But when he pitches a curve or a slider, he brings certain nerves and muscles into strained or unnatural movements. Similar strains are involved in the playing of many instruments. Musicians who have the most problems, because of the physical agility and long hours of practice required, are string players. Then piano players and woodwind players. The least afflicted are percussionists. Although I did have one once—a big, powerful rock drummer. He played his drums like a jackhammer operator, and his trouble was simply overuse. He had calluses an eighth of an inch thick on his fingers. I'll give you an example I often use. A typical full-size violin measures twenty-five point five to twenty-five point eight centimeters from the bridge to the nut—the ridge the strings pass over at the top of the neck—and that defines the maximum length of the vibrating string. About two and a half octaves can be played on the high-pitched E string. Overtones, or harmonics, played on the same string increase the number of notes. The distance that the finger must be moved along the string to play the next higher note decreases as the pitch rises. This adds complexity to the task. Minute errors in finger placement cause the note to be out of tune, and similarly small deviations in the coordination between the bow and the finger placement cause the note to be too short, too long, or imprecise. Absolutely precise negotiation of these small differences of movement is what distinguishes the technique of a Heifetz from that of an ordinary violinist. Or that of a great pianist from the merely competent. In playing a Beethoven piano sonata, literally thousands of notes must be struck in the space of just a few minutes, and struck, of course, with absolutely precise use of joint flexion, extension, and rotation.

"These are simply the basic demands that confront every instrumentalist. Perfection doesn't come easy. But there are a multitude of accidental or arbitrary problems as well. I remember a patient, a woman violinist, who came to me with a very painful right wrist—her bow wrist. It was clearly a case of tendinitis. It turned out that she had recently bought a new violin, and was testing a new bow. She had some difficulty at first in finding the sound she wanted, but she worked at it, and finally got it right, and that was when her trouble began. The new violin, and the new bow, too, were apparently slightly different in construction from her previous ones. She had had to put more physical effort into getting results that satisfied her. When I examined her, I found a microscopic trauma in her wrist. It had probably developed after only a few days of that unusual effort, but the damage was severe enough to force her to rest for three or four months. She would have been much better off if she had broken her wrist—a fracture would have mended in around six weeks. Cellists and double bass players have the same potential for neuromuscular injury, and more. The cello and the double bass are heavy and awkward instruments that require more pure physical strength to play. And clarinetists: one of their problems lies in the nature of the instrument. A clarinet weighs almost two pounds, and its entire weight in supported by one thumb. Along with everything else, a clarinetist needs a strong and enduring thumb.

"There are probably as many as a hundred and thirty thousand instrumentalists in the United States who play for a living. There are also some forty-eight symphony orchestras, and they employ only about three percent of those musicians—just over four thousand of them. Whatever the statistics, it is obvious that there are a great many musicians competing for a very limited number of jobs. To compete for—to even hope for—one of those jobs, a musician must be much better than merely good. That means, of course, hours of practice every day. Most of my patients are people who have overdone it, many of them young conservatory students. It is those desperate extra hours of practice, of striving to make an impression, of repeating a difficult phrase over and over again that fills our consulting rooms. I think my son Daniel has learned not to overdo it. At any rate, I'm there to watch him. I had a young violist who was scheduled to perform before a jury in the early spring, and he decided to use the Christmas vacation to get in some real practicing. He started out working four to six hours a day, and drove himself up to eight and ten, and even more. Then, of course, he had to stop: he was in agony. It was weeks before he could play again. I had another young patient whose teacher—his teacher!—told him not to bother with warming up—just pick up your instrument and start playing! That was incredibly bad advice. Musicians aren't that different from athletes. A warmup means just that. The body needs warmth to function well. When a player comes into the practice room from a walk in the cold, or into an air-conditioned room, he must give his body time to generate the proper muscle temperature. I tell my patients to pay attention to the tightening feeling that means fatigue. Take a rest. Take a five-minute rest every half hour. Those five minutes can be used to rehearse mentally. The mind can hear as well as the ear.

"Tendinitis and other problems that result from overuse usually respond to simple rest. Anti-inflammatory drugs are sometimes indicated during the acute stage. When that stage has passed, rest is combined with carefully designed exercises to stretch and strengthen the muscle-tendon unit. But the amount of blood supplied to the tendons is low, and severe cases may require as long as eight months for full recovery. Unusually severe cases—cases, perhaps, in which pain was long ignored—may develop into a serious condition called dystonia. Dystonia is a loss of muscle control. The whole body can be affected, or only a part. The dystonia we see here is generally a focal dystonia, which means that the deterioration is focused on a certain muscle or muscle group. In our clinic, that most often involves the wrists or the hands or the fingers. The most familiar form of dystonia was recognized many years ago, and is known as writer's cramp. The usual presenting sign of focal dystonia is incoordination, possibly accompanied by an involuntary curling of a finger or fingers. I remember a rock guitarist. He had all the expected symptoms of tendinitis, and also an uncontrollable left little finger. At any time in the course of a performance it would suddenly curl under the neck, the fingerboard, of his guitar. He had tried everything before he finally gave up and came to us. He had even tried tying the finger back, to keep it out of the way. I saw him only once. He never returned for another appointment. In any event, treatment involves the use of antispasmodic drugs, and the results have been very disappointing. Focal dystonia has ended some great careers. The pianists Gary Graffman and Leon Fleisher are among its victims, and there is good evidence that Robert Schumann was also one. When I talked with Mary-Margaret Carden's husband and arranged for a consultation, I was afraid that she might be another."

On July 11, 1988, Dr. Lockwood met Miss Carden in his consulting room at the clinic for what turned out to be the first of several visits. He had requested, and received, the considerable chart compiled by her numerous Fort Smith physicians, and his preliminary routine physical examination ("She was a well-developed, healthy, well-nourished-looking woman who appeared to be her stated age . . .") confirmed the general spectrum of those earlier findings. Then, as is his custom with ailing instrumentalists, he sat Miss Carden down at her instrument—in this case (the clinic not having an organ) a piano—and asked her to play for him. It was a revealing command performance. He noted on her chart: "The lack of precision she described in playing was quite evident in playing even simple music or scales. To my eye and ear, this seemed to be more extensive than involving just the ring and small fingers, which she identified as the only abnormal digits, although the action of these 2 fingers was slower than would be expected. Specifically, she was unable to play trills with the ring and small finger of the right hand, a task that had been quite simple in the past. There were no clear-cut dystonic postures observable, although on occasion, in the left hand, her small finger protruded in an unusual fashion. No curling or other finger-position abnormalities were evident. She states that her hand will shake after playing, and a fine essential tremor-like movement was seen. I believe that . . . it is likely she has mild ulnar-entrapment neuropathies at the wrist at Guyon's canal [an area on the palmar eminence opposite the thumb], more marked on the right than on the left. I am also somewhat concerned . . . that she may be developing a focal dystonia."

Miss Carden went back to Arkansas as disabled as ever but much improved in spirit. "Dr. Lockwood was wonderful," she says. "He talked to me. He listened to what I had to say, and he took the trouble to hear me play. He understood me as a musician. He wanted to see me again, in a month or so. He wanted me to have another EMG, and at the time of my menstrual period, so I was to set the date. The idea was that the stress and fluid retention at the time of menstruation might exacerbate my trouble, and he wanted to study it at its worst. He seemed to know what he was doing. He seemed to be able to make up his mind. I looked forward to that next visit." That visit took place in early September. The EMG examination was performed as planned, and the results showed no evidence of improvement or alleviation. Miss Carden was again observed at the piano, and "the suspected abnormalities of finger position observed last time seemed more clean-cut." Dr. Lockwood arrived at a decision. He recorded on her chart: "I tend to favor exploration of Guyon's canal with the following rationale. I believe that she has ulnar-nerve symptomology—electrical evidence in the past has shown distal latencies [sluggish transmission] of the sensory portion of the nerve. Early surgery for nerve compression may . . . inhibit or reverse symptoms of early focal dystonias. . . . Although there can be no assurance of success, I think it's reasonable to explore the right hand with these objectives in mind."

The surgery on Miss Carden's right hand was performed some weeks later by a hand surgeon named David Hildreth. The operation, though delicate, was superficial in scope, and required only a local anesthetic. Miss Carden's recovery, in medical parlance, was "uneventful," and the operation fully achieved its aim. The source of her pain had been found and removed. Dr. Lockwood noted on her chart, "She is extremely pleased. . . . In fact, she refers to her hand as having 'been given back to her.'" This success encouraged Dr. Lockwood to propose a similar operation on her left hand. Miss Carden and her husband readily agreed, and a similar torturing fibrous band was found and similarly removed by Dr. John T. Burns, in January 1989. In a brief informal note to Dr. Lockwood, Dr. Burns reported, "Miss Carden underwent surgical decompression of the left ulnar nerve at Guyon's canal. . . . Indeed, a fibrous band overlying and compressing the motor branch of the ulnar nerve was noted, and appropriately released." Its release was actually a severing. The fibrous tissue constricting the nerve was snipped apart with a pair of tenotomy scissors. Her recovery, as before, was comfortable and complete. A few months later, she found that she could again play the organ, and without discomfort, and was once more capable of full-time work among the azaleas.

Dr. Lockwood's original suspicion of an emerging focal dystonia was mistaken. There was no dystonia. His was, however, a fortunate error—the abnormal hand movements were caused by the compressed nerve. The hand is a fragile mosaic of nerves and tendons, and had it not been for that suspicion, it is probable that he would have decided against the risk of surgery. "As a matter of fact," Dr. Lockwood says, "her trouble was really quite a rarity. Those bands were an anomaly—and, I think, a congenital anomaly. They may have always been there, and if she had led a different kind of life their presence might never have been known. She wrenched them alive with her hands. She made them draw and tighten. If she hadn't been an organist, and if she hadn't also worked in a nursery, and if she hadn't, on top of that, done a lot of typing—well, the combination was just too much."

# Hoping

Norah Sullivan, as I'll call her, first became aware
that there was something wrong with her leg—
her right thigh—on the morning of Tuesday, December 10, 1991. It was sore, and it ached. Miss Sullivan had just that month turned thirty, and she was
comfortably situated as a nanny in the home of a family in the West New Brighton section of the New York
City borough of Staten Island. Her leg continued to
ache throughout the day, but she went to bed with the
natural hope that it would be all right in the morning.
It wasn't. It was worse, and it more than ached. It
hurt, it hurt sitting, and even lying down. And it was
even more painful on Thursday. It seemed swollen,
inflamed, and sensitive to the touch. That night after

dinner, at the suggestion of her employers, she walked (walking was her least painful posture) around to the office of a neighborhood physician who kept evening hours. He looked at her leg, examined it with care. His impression, whatever it was, he kept to himself. He must, however, have been impressed. He told her he felt that she needed treatment of a sort that he was unable to provide. The place for her, he said, was the hospital, and he advised her to go there at once.

The hospital to which he referred is St. Vincent's Medical Center of Richmond, a teaching affiliate of New York Medical College, in Valhalla, New York. St. Vincent's was founded, as St. Vincent's Hospital, before the turn of the last century and is something of a landmark in that part of Staten Island. It has grown over the years, in generational jumps, to a five-story complex occupying a large city block, but the original red brick nineteenth-century building, with its elegant interior—walnut paneling, eighteen-foot ceilings, mosaic tile floors—is still in good repair and in use. The emergency room, where Miss Sullivan presented herself at around nine-thirty, is of more recent construction and contemporaneously functional.

"I'm here because of my leg," Miss Sullivan told the receptionist. "It hurts."

The receptionist responded with professional sympathy, and then elicited the standard information—name, address, age, religion, social security number, method of payment. Miss Sullivan was directed to an examination cubicle, where she was received by an emergency service physician. Her complaint?

"I'm here because of my leg," she said. "It hurts."

He settled her on an examination table. He studied

her leg, her swollen thigh. It *looked* painful. And, as a gentle manipulation demonstrated, it was tender to the touch. He asked her to move her leg, and to roll over; she did so, and winced. A possible, an even probable, diagnosis entered the doctor's mind, and settled unpleasantly there, but he proceeded with the prescribed procedure. She was a well-developed, well-nourished white female, who looked her stated age. There was no family history of diabetes or of peptic ulcer. Her father, aged fifty-four, had had some muscular problem with his legs; her mother, aged fifty-one, had had a heart attack, but appeared to have recovered. She herself had undergone an appendectomy at age twelve. She didn't smoke. She enjoyed an occasional drink. She had never used an oral contraceptive. He moved on to the physical examination. Her blood pressure was satisfactory—98/70. Her temperature was slightly elevated—it read 100.3ffl. His findings were otherwise unremarkable. The triage system of patient classification is practiced at St. Vincent's. It identifies patients who need no treatment, patients who are to be treated and released, and patients whose treatment requires hospitalization. The emergency room physician placed Miss Sullivan in the third category. The next step was to arrange for her admission. He summoned the admitting physician on duty that night, and the two doctors conferred. Miss Sullivan's leg was reexamined. The emergency room physician offered his diagnostic suspicion—a deep vein thrombosis. His colleague concurred. The hospital records show that she was admitted at 10:10 P.M. She asked for a telephone, and called her employers and told them where she was and why. She was then rolled up to a dormitory ward and put to bed. But not, of course, to sleep.

A deep vein thrombosis is an obstruction in a deep-lying vein which is caused by an accumulation of clotted blood. This can occur in either arms or legs, but its usual site is the leg, most commonly the thigh. A deep vein thrombosis in the leg is always, and uniquely, signaled by pain. Two factors are involved in the formation of a thrombotic clot. One is a predisposing sluggish flow of blood through one part of the body. The other is some physiological event that unnaturally stimulates the natural protective phenomenon of coagulation. The normal flow of blood tends to slow when one lies or sits for long periods of time, as in bed rest following surgery or in chronic illness. A sluggish flow of blood may also be generated by congestive heart failure, varicose veins, obesity, oral contraceptives, old age, smoking, and trauma. A deep vein thrombosis is not in itself of serious significance, but it has a serious potential. The ever-present danger in a thrombosis is that a fragment or fragments of the clot may break loose and be carried in the circulation to the heart and from there to the lungs. The resulting pulmonary embolism is always a major medical emergency, and not infrequently fatal. Pulmonary embolism claims around fifty thousand victims in the United States each year; most of these, for reasons not entirely clear, are women.

The presence of a deep vein thrombosis, though easily suspected, is not easily established by physical examination alone. An apodictic diagnosis can be achieved only by a visualizing technology called venography. This procedure consists of the introduction of some radiopaque substance into the patient's veins and subsequent examination by X ray. A thrombosis, if present, will pictorially declare itself. The treatment of deep vein thrombosis is pragmatically direct. Its purpose is to dissolve and eliminate the obstructing coagulated blood and to prevent its recurrence. There are several effective anticoagulant drugs available to the clinician. The oldest of these (discovered in 1916) is a chemical complexity called heparin, and it is still probably the most widely preferred. The chief reason for this is that its action is both therapeutic and prophylactic and is quick, almost instantaneous. Its only drawback is that it must be administered parenterally, by continuous intravenous delivery. The newer anticoagulants can be taken orally, a considerable convenience, but they are distressingly slow to exert their strength—their impact is never felt in less than eighteen hours. The admitting physician noted on Miss Sullivan's chart an order for prompt heparin therapy.

Miss Sullivan's hospital night was no less uncomfortable than the night before at home. Her leg continued to hurt. She had hoped for some pain relief, but that was denied her. The analgesics in common use—aspirin, ibuprofen, naproxen, Tylenol—all share to a limited degree the anticoagulating powers of heparin; any one of these drugs in combination with heparin incurs the risk of hemorrhage. Her rest was otherwise disturbed. She was hardly settled in bed when a nurse and a technician appeared and affixed the apparatus necessary for the intravenous administration of heparin. Nor was that all. She experienced in full the nocturnal attentions traditional to hospital life. A nurse appeared from time to time with a blood-pressure cuff or a clinical thermometer or to monitor the IV's measured drip. Then, at some later early hour, she was aroused once more and transported to a laboratory where the indicated X-ray diagnostic procedure was performed. She was returned to the ward for a round of ablutions, and breakfast. At around nine o'clock, she opened her eyes to the smiling face of a tall and attractive young woman in the short white coat and pocketed stethoscope of authority.

This was Susan Balog, an intern assigned that month to that service. Miss Sullivan was the last of some eight or ten patients whom Dr. Balog had seen in the ward that morning. She saw in this new patient a drawn face and an undemonstrative manner. She asked her how she felt.

"I'm here because of my leg," Miss Sullivan said. "It hurts."

Dr. Balog examined the painful leg. Its movement was clearly limited by pain. Miss Sullivan, nevertheless, lay uncomplaining. She was, Dr. Balog noted, of stoical temperament. She was somewhat stocky, of sturdy, athletic build; her thighs were heavy, but muscular rather than fat. She was pleasantly plain. Dr. Balog continued her examination, and found nothing remarkable. She reviewed Miss Sullivan's chart. The results of the standard tests and soundings reported there were with one exception reassuringly normal. The exception was her white-blood-cell count. It was somewhat elevated—11,700 per cubic millimeters. Normal is around 7,500. An elevated white-cell count is a sign of infection. The elevation in this case was more confusing than suggestive. There was a recent notation on the chart, from the radiologist who had studied Miss Sullivan's venogram. He had found no evidence of a thrombosis. Her femoral vein was in no way obstructed. Dr. Balog gave orders that the heparin therapy be discontinued, and since it also now seemed safe to provide Miss Sullivan with a further measure of ease, prescribed a course of naproxin—250 to 500 milligrams twice a day. She offered Miss Sullivan some words of comfort and encouragement, and continued on her appointed rounds. The normal venogram was, of course, welcome good news. It eliminated a dark and unsettling explanation. But that was all. The cause of Miss Sullivan's painful thigh was once more a problem requiring prompt resolution.

Dr. Balog returned to Miss Sullivan's ward and bedside an hour or two later, at around eleven o'clock. This time, she was in company. She was a member of the entourage that accompanied Dr. Michael Phillips, associate director of medicine at St. Vincent's Medical Center and professor of clinical medicine at New York Medical College, on his regular morning rounds. Dr. Phillips is in his middle forties, of good height and posture, dark-haired and dark-eyed, with a broad, untroubled face and the crisp remains of an English accent. He was born in England, but emigrated with his parents to Australia, where he graduated in medicine from the University of Western Australia, in Perth. He also had fellowship training in clinical pharmacology at the University of California in San Francisco. I talked with him not long ago in his office in the center's original building—a beautifully proportioned and finished room of almost museum quality, with a view through the door of a wide and lofty corridor and a resplendent fireplace of hand-carved stone. The case of Norah Sullivan is one that he easily recalls, and with a somewhat ironic satisfaction.

"I don't have a private practice," Dr. Phillips told me. "The patients I see are here, in the hospital. I see most of them for the first time on rounds. I met Norah Sullivan for the first time that Friday morning. Friday the thirteenth. Dr. Balog presented the patient. She reviewed the history, the workup, the findings. She did it well. It was easy to understand what had been done, and why—the possibility of a deep vein thrombosis must be taken seriously. But now the venogram had ruled it out. So what to do next? I was the attending physician. It was my responsibility. The poor young woman was in pain, and I'm quite sure she was feeling a bit anxious. But, as Dr. Balog had noted, she was pleasant and uncomplaining. We don't see too many stoics. I'm not one of those who like to order tests. I don't believe in doing something just out of academic interest. My rule of thumb is to order a test only when the result can bring about a change in the management of the patient. I require a darn good reason for everything we do. But something had to be done about Miss Sullivan. We stood there scratching our heads. If it wasn't a deep vein thrombosis, what else could produce those symptoms? A pelvic tumor? That was a thought. A pelvic tumor can compress a blood vessel in a way that mimics a thrombosis. That was certainly something we had better find out about. So I said let's get a gynecological assessment and an orthopedic opinion.

"Meanwhile, I had had a good look at her thigh. It was very tender and red and swollen. And now I had a sudden thought, an impulse. You probably know the classic medical saying: When you hear hoofbeats, you don't necessarily think of a zebra. I'm one of those who listen to what they hear. I'm always ready to be amazed. I asked Miss Sullivan if she did a lot of exercising—she rather had that build. She said, Oh, yes. She liked all kinds of sports activity. I wondered if she had been doing any unusual exercising recently. She seemed to think for a minute, and then she said, Well, yes—she guessed she had. She had been using a mechanical device that was supposed to thin her thighs. She thought her thighs were too heavy. I thought, Ah ha! Did I hear zebras come galloping across the plain? I said tell me more. She had bought the device by mail. It was a padded, springlike contrivance held between the knees; when you opened and closed your thighs, that provided resistance. It was supposed to make for shapely thighs. She said she had been using it for about six weeks, every day for fifteen minutes. She acted it out, showed me in pantomime how the device worked. I had never heard of it. She said she had the thing at home, and I asked her to ask someone to bring it over here. I wanted to see it to believe it. When I got home that night, I described the device to my wife and daughter. Had they ever heard of it? They stared at me. Of course they knew about it. It was advertised in the papers and magazines. And it was promoted on television by a gorgeous TV star. Well!"

Dr. Phillips paused. Perhaps he was listening again to those distant zebra hoofbeats. I could appreciate that it isn't always easy to remember the surge and sequence of a moment of inspiration. He said, "I think I was reasonably satisfied at that point. Hard and regular use of that exercise device was a persuasive explanation of her painful thigh. There was a study back in 1980 in the *British Journal of Sports Medicine* that examined injuries among athletes. It found that loading of the adductor muscles during intensive training may lead to injury and inflammation in the region of the adductor origins. Adductor muscles are those that draw or pull a limb back toward its normal position, and in this context they would be those that move the upper leg. That was a sustaining thought. But, of course, it would have been most unwise not to go on—not to look around a bit more. There was nothing more that could be done for Miss Sullivan at the moment. Naproxen would be having the expected effect. She would be starting to feel less uncomfortable. While we were waiting for the X-ray studies of her hip and femur, I reviewed the remaining reasonable possibilities. There was a rheumatoid factor to consider to rule out rheumatoid arthritis. Meanwhile, somebody—one of Miss Sullivan's friends or a member of the family she worked for—brought us the exercise device. It was just as she had described it, and she demonstrated it for us. Unfortunately it went back home with Miss Sullivan, though I do have one of the print advertisements for it—you'll find it interesting reading. But I don't want to get too far ahead of myself.

"We're still talking about Friday the thirteenth. Things began to fall very quickly in place. First, the possibility of a tumor was eliminated. Here's a summary of the gynecologist's report: 'GYN evaluation with abdominal ultrasound did not give information to support physical findings associated with GYN problems.' The discharge summary tells the rest of the story: 'Orthopedic consultation gave impression for acute synovitis of right hip with recommendation of CT scan to be performed. This was done and showed fluid collection in the right hip joint. Rheumatology consult agreed with above. . . . Rheumatoid factor was negative. . . . Final diagnosis: Tenosynovitis of right hip.' Tenosynovitis is an inflammation of the lining that surrounds a tendon. The cause, the usual cause, is excessive friction brought on by overuse. My own diagnosis—my little contribution to the literature—is a bit more explicit. I called it thigh-thinner's thecitis. And that was the happy end of the story, except that Miss Sullivan stayed with us for almost another week—it took that long for her condition to stabilize. We were finally able to discharge her on Thursday, December the nineteenth."

Something had been bothering me from earlier in our conversation. It came into my mind with Dr. Phillips's first mention of the exercising device and his description of how it worked. This seemed a good time to voice it. How come, I said, if both legs were involved in the push and pull of the exercise, how come only the right leg was affected?

Dr. Phillips nodded. "That's a good question," he said. "I wish I could give you an absolute answer. The best I can do is this. None of our extremities, none of our duplicated body parts, are exactly symmetrical. Most of us, as any shoe salesman can tell you, have feet that don't perfectly match. I can only suppose that there was something about her right leg, some little weakness, that made it more susceptible to strain and injury."

He felt through some papers on his desk, and came up with a large advertisement in full and commanding color. He handed it to me with an anticipatory smile. "Anyway," he said. "Here's the culprit."

I put on my glasses, and looked. My eyes, as intended, were immediately struck by a photograph of a young woman, blond and beautiful, with a firm and flawless figure, reclining in a pose strongly and fierily suggestive of Madame Récamier. She spoke to me through a headline: NOW YOU CAN HAVE SHAPELY THIGHS IN JUST MINUTES A DAY! Another exhortation read, "Just squeeze your way to a firmer, shapelier you!" And, "Easy-to-follow instructions show you how to isolate 'problem' areas." And, "Strengthens and tones exactly where you need it most." And, finally, "You'll also receive . . . my easy weight-loss menu plan." It was priced at $19.95.

"Well," Dr. Phillips said. "Rather a cruel hoax, wouldn't you say?"

I agreed. But, I suggested, it was also very clever. It carefully avoided the actually fraudulent. It made no promises of thinner thighs. The word "thin" was never used. There was only "firmer" and "shapelier" and "strengthens" and "tones." Nevertheless, a thinning effect was certainly implied.

"Quite," Dr. Phillips said. "But the only result, if any, of using the device would be just the opposite. I tried to make that clear to Miss Sullivan when I explained the cause of her trouble. I gave her a little lecture on physiology. One can selectively develop muscle—look at all those weight-lifters. But one cannot selectively eliminate fat. Fat can be eliminated only through an all-over reduction in weight, and that can be achieved only by a reduced intake of food, by dieting. Miss Sullivan's exercises not only put her in the hospital. They also, if anything, *enlarged* her thighs. They made them more muscular."

I wondered how she had received the lecture.

"That's a little hard to say," he said. "She seemed to accept it all very philosophically. I had a sense, though, that she was confused and disappointed. She had very much hoped it would work."

Did he think that he had convinced her?

"I wonder," he said. "She took the device home with her. She might very well try it again. Hope is a powerful thing. Springs eternal, and all that. Look at those expensive antiwrinkle creams. Those hair restorers. I often think of Samuel Johnson when he heard that a friend whose nagging wife had died was getting married for the second time. Second marriages, he told Boswell, are the triumph of hope over experience."

# A Woman
# with a Headache

A woman I'll call Mildred Anderson—Mrs. Harold Anderson—was admitted to Temple University Hospital, in North Philadelphia, on the afternoon of Friday, January 19, 1968, for observation and treatment of a severe and persistent headache. Mrs. Anderson's admission was arranged by Dr. Albert J. Finestone, an internist and a clinical professor of medicine at Temple University School of Medicine, to whom she had been referred by her family physician, and she was shown to a two-bed room on the fourth floor and made as comfortable as possible. That was around two o'clock. At five, an intern on Dr. Finestone's service named Mary E. Moore dropped in for the opening diagnostic interrogation.

Dr. Moore introduced herself. She sat down and smiled and asked Mrs. Anderson how she felt. Mrs. Anderson said she felt pretty good. She hesitated. As a matter of fact, she felt fine. It was a funny thing, she said. It was almost embarrassing. Her headache was gone. In the two or three hours that she had been in the hospital, it had completely vanished. She didn't understand it at all. It was almost as if the hospital had scared it away. Dr. Moore said nothing. She nodded and made a sympathetic sound. But she thought she understood it well enough. Dr. Moore is not only a doctor of medicine. She is also a doctor of philosophy in experimental psychology, and she knew that it was entirely possible that Mrs. Anderson's headache *had* been scared away. Hospitals often have that effect on functional, or psychogenic, disorders. That didn't mean, however, that Mrs. Anderson's headache *was* functional in origin. It was just a possibility. Hospitals often momentarily exert much the same inhibiting effect on the pain of disorders that are fully and ferociously somatic.

Dr. Moore got out her pen and a ruled personal-history form. Mrs. Anderson was a striking-looking woman. Her hair was white, her complexion was rough and florid, and her eyes were large and expressive. She was small and notably thin. Her age, as given on her chart, was forty-one. The chart also noted that she and her husband, a civil engineer, were childless, and owned their own home. Mrs. Anderson shifted her position in bed—and Dr. Moore was startled to see that her spine was twisted and bent in the hump-backed conformation known as kyphoscoliosis. Startled and interested. That explained Mrs. Anderson's size, and possibly more than that. Dr. Moore began the interview. Mrs. Anderson was quietly and politely responsive. Her chief complaint was, of course, a headache. It had first appeared about three weeks ago. She had suffered off and on for many years from what she believed were migraine headaches, but this was nothing like those. There was no nausea, no vomiting, no sensitivity to light. It was simply an excruciating pain that progressed from the back of her head to the top. The migraine headaches had begun in childhood, and she was the only member of her family to be so afflicted. The only drug she ever took was aspirin—until recently. Three weeks ago, her doctor prescribed a drug called Fiorinal for her headache. Dr. Moore nodded. Fiorinal is a popular, non-narcotic sedative and analgesic. However, Mrs. Anderson said, it hadn't done much good. This was the first real relief she had had in all those weeks. It was also her first experience as a hospital patient. Her back was not the result of either illness or injury: she had been born that way. She had never been seriously ill, and she had no known allergies. She drank occasionally, but she didn't smoke. Her ruddy complexion was normal for her. Her skin was naturally very dry. It was often blotchy, and it tended to redden whenever she was tense or nervous. She had been like that all her life. Was she nervous now? Well, yes—she supposed she was. After all, she had never been hospitalized before.

That completed the historical phase of the interview. Dr. Moore moved from her chair to the bedside, and began the customary routine physical examination. She identified Mrs. Anderson's chronic dermatitis as ichthyosis congenita. She found Mrs. Anderson's eyes, ears, nose, throat, and neck to be essentially normal. There was no ocular evidence of brain tumor or of any intracranial swelling, and no venous distension, and no thyroid- or lymph-gland enlargement. She confirmed her snap diagnosis of kyphoscoliosis. Mrs. Anderson's breasts were normal. Her heart was normal in size and rhythm, and her lungs were clear to auscultation and percussion. There were no discernible abdominal masses, and her liver and spleen felt normal. Her reflexes were satisfactory, as were the results of a careful neurological examination. Dr. Moore added these reassuring but unilluminating findings to the record. She then turned to the order sheet and noted down the several preliminary tests and studies that she wished to have made. They included blood analyses (hematocrit, hemoglobin, serology, blood sugar, kidney function), urinalysis, chest X-ray, spine X-ray, neck X-ray, skull X-ray, brain scan, electroencephalogram, and electrocardiogram. The results of one or another of these should produce at least a glimmer of diagnostic enlightenment. Dr. Moore also asked that a dermatologist be consulted about the treatment of Mrs. Anderson's ichthyosis. She further noted that Mrs. Anderson was to be given codeine as needed (thirty milligrams every four hours) for the relief of her headache, and Nembutal (one hundred milligrams) for sleep. She closed the preliminary report with a preliminary comment: "Impression: (1) Congenital kyphoscoliosis. (2) Congenital ichthyosis. (3) Headache of unknown etiology—probably cervical spine deformity as cause. To be ruled out: Brain tumor or other intracerebral lesion."

Mrs. Anderson spent a generally comfortable night. She slept with the help of Nembutal, but she had no need for codeine. Her headache was still ambiguously quiescent. She was rested but not yet fully relaxed when Dr. Finestone walked in on his rounds the following morning with his entourage of students and interns. Dr. Finestone was roughly familiar with the nature of her case. He had spoken with Dr. Moore the night before, and he had just now read her notes and comments. Nevertheless, like all scrupulous attending physicians, he sat down and saw for himself. He led Mrs. Anderson briefly back through her relevant history, and then appraised by direct examination what her history suggested were the physical essentials. He was interested and puzzled by the disappearance of her headache. But he could see no cause for any alarm, and he ended the visit with a word of sincere reassurance.

The next day—January 21st—was a Sunday. It passed aggreeably for Mrs. Anderson. She had a visit from her husband, and there was still no return of her headache. An intern on weekend duty noted that she seemed less tense and restless than reported the day before. The strangeness of the hospital life appeared to be wearing off. On Monday, the first results of the diagnostic studies were reported. They included the standard laboratory tests, the electrocardiogram, and three of the four requested X-ray examinations— chest, neck, and spine. Dr. Finestone and Dr. Moore went over the findings together. None of the reports contained any diagnostic surprises. Mrs. Anderson's chest, heart, kidneys, and blood were normal. The radiologist's report on the look of her neck and spine read: "A marked degree of scoliosis of the dorsal spine with the convexity to the right is seen. . . . Changes in the thorax secondary to scoliosis are also noted. The cervical and dorsal spine reveal no other significant abnormalities. The intervertebral foramina are patent. No osteolytic or osteoblastic abnormalities are seen." (Osteolysis is a dissolution of bone, and an osteoblast is a cell involved in bone production.) Later that day, the dermatological consultant confirmed that Mrs. Anderson's skin condition was indeed a congenital ichthyosis, and prescribed for its correction a regimen of oil baths and rubs.

Two of the three remaining studies were completed on Wednesday. They were the skull X-ray and the electroencephalogram. Dr. Finestone recorded the results on Mrs. Anderson's chart: "EEG & skull films negative." He then added his comments and conclusions: "Pain gone. Likely diagnosis—cervical spondylosis. Doubt intracranial cause." The results of the brain-scan study were reported the following day. They considerably decreased the possibility of any cerebral involvement: "Following administration of technetium 99m pertechnetate, the brain was examined by the scintillation camera in five views (anterior, posterior, left lateral, right lateral, and vertex) after preparation with potassium perchlorate. No abnormalities are noted in any of these views." That was the last of the diagnostic studies, and it seemed to Dr. Moore almost conclusive. It strengthened her impression that there was nothing very wrong with Mrs. Anderson. Even the woman's headache was gone—spontaneously gone—and had been gone for close to a week. Dr. Moore noted on the chart for Dr. Finestone's approval that Mrs. Anderson was now ready for discharge. Dr. Finestone concurred in this judgment, and Mrs. Anderson was discharged from the hospital early on Thursday afternoon. Her case was closed with a final diagnosis: "Headache secondary to cervical scoliosis and nervous tension."

Dr. Moore was with Mrs. Anderson when her husband arrived to take her home. Mr. Anderson was much like his wife—quiet, pleasant, cooperative. He was also, like his wife, a little confused and worried. They didn't understand that equivocal week in the hospital. Dr. Moore undertook to reassure them. She reminded Mrs. Anderson of the many tests and examinations that she had undergone. They were the reason for her protracted hospital stay. She then explained their uniform results. There was no cause for any concern. Just the reverse. The tests had made it clear that Mrs. Anderson was in enviably excellent health. Dr. Moore tried to speak with conviction, and the Andersons were convinced. They thanked her and shook her hand and left the hospital arm in arm. Dr. Moore went on to her other patients. Some of them might never be discharged, and Mrs. Anderson dropped untroubled from her mind.

Dr. Finestone was the first to have Mrs. Anderson recalled to his attention. She was returned to his mind at one o'clock on Friday afternoon by another telephone call. The call reached him at Temple University Hospital, and the caller was Mr. Anderson. He was apologetically distraught. He was calling about his wife. When he had brought her home from the hospital on Thursday afternoon she seemed to be in good spirits and she said she was feeling fine. He left her at home and went down to his office to finish up some urgent work. When he got back to the house a couple of hours later, she was prostrate on the sofa with one of her terrible headaches. He telephoned their doctor, and the doctor came to the house and gave her an injection of Demerol. That helped her through the night. But the headache came back this morning, and now—just a few minutes ago—his wife had fainted. He had come home from his office for lunch to see how she was. She told him she was feeling sick and dizzy, and that was when she fainted. She was conscious now, but she looked as if she might pass out again any minute. What should he do? Dr. Finestone asked if he called the family doctor again. No? Then Mr. Anderson should call him, and right away. He was their regular doctor, he lived in the neighborhood, and he had treated Mrs. Anderson only the night before. However, if Mr. Anderson couldn't reach the doctor, he was to call Dr. Finestone again and bring his wife to the hospital. Mr. Anderson thanked him, and Dr. Finestone hung up and resumed his interrupted rounds. He wondered what could have happened to Mrs. Anderson. He couldn't relate it to anything in her known condition of health. It was very strange. It almost sounded hysterical. But she hadn't impressed him as being that neurotic. He finished his rounds, and Mr. Anderson still hadn't called. It was safe to assume that the matter was now in the hands of the family doctor. He looked around for Dr. Moore. It would be interesting to hear her opinion. But she wasn't on the floor. Dr. Finestone went down and changed out of his long white coat and put on his overcoat and went home. He didn't see Dr. Moore again until Sunday. By then it was all over.

Dr. Moore was assigned to overnight duty on Saturday. She reported to the hospital at noon and spent the afternoon on the floor. There were old patients to see and new patients to meet and study. She had dinner in the hospital cafeteria at five o'clock, and then went back to continue with her patients and see them settled for the night. It was an undemanding evening on her floor, and around midnight she went down to the emergency room and joined a couple of other idling interns and the resident on duty there. She had been sitting in their company about an hour—smoking and talking and drinking coffee—when she heard herself being paged. She walked around the corner to the house telephone. The call was not a summons from her floor. It was an outside call. The caller was a young woman and her voice was shrill and excited.

"Is this Dr. Mary Moore?"

"Yes."

"I'm the niece of Mrs. Anderson. One of her nieces. I think you helped take care of her when she was in the hospital?"

"That's right."

"Well, I'm over here at her house. At the Andersons' house. I came over this evening because my uncle called and asked me to help, and something terrible has happened to her. It's awful. She had this terrible headache yesterday, and she passed out I don't know how many times—and now she's lost the power of the tendons in her legs."

Dr. Moore stood silent with the telephone in her hand. She was stunned. She couldn't believe it. Mrs. Anderson had spent a full week under careful observation in a first-class university teaching hospital, and according to the most sophisticated tests and tabulations she was in essentially the best of health. There had been no sign of any serious ailment. But now— just two days later—she . . .

Dr. Moore took a deep breath. "You mean she's paralyzed?"

"I guess that's what it is," the niece said. "She's lost the power of her tendons."

"I think I'd better speak to Mrs. Anderson. Can you get her to the phone?"

"I'm afraid you can't. I mean, it wouldn't do any good. She isn't making any sense."

"Then let me speak to Mr. Anderson."

"My uncle?" She gave a wild laugh. "He's acting just as crazy as she is."

"Oh," Dr. Moore said. But she also felt a kind of relief. If both of the Andersons were affected, it must be something that had happened after Mrs. Anderson left the hospital. It might be some deranging form of food poisoning. It might be drugs. It might be simple alcohol. She remembered that Mrs. Anderson liked an occasional drink. "Do you think they might be drunk?"

"I don't know," the niece said. "I don't think so. I don't see any glasses or bottle or anything." She gave another wild laugh. "My uncle fainted this afternoon. That was before he called me."

Dr. Moore hesitated. She wondered if the niece had

been drinking. "How about you?" she said. "Are you all right?"

"I don't know," the niece said. "I guess so. Sure, I'm O.K."

"I hope so," Dr. Moore said. "I want your aunt and uncle at the hospital as soon as possible. Can you get them here? Do you need any help?"

"I don't need any help. My friends have a car. I've got some friends here with me. I guess I forgot to tell you that. They're an older couple I know."

"All right," Dr. Moore said. "Come to the emergency room. I'll meet you there."

"O.K.," the niece said.

Dr. Moore waited at the emergency-room door. It opened and closed on the regular Saturday-night procession of beatings and knifings and car-wreck lacerations. At a little past two, the car with the niece and her friends and her aunt and uncle pulled into the curb, and Dr. Moore sent an orderly out to meet them with a rolling stretcher. She watched him lifting Mrs. Anderson onto the stretcher and the rest of them milling around and trying to help. Mr. Anderson wore striped pajamas under his overcoat, and he seemed to be yelling. The orderly pushed the stretcher up the walk and into the foyer, and Mrs. Anderson lifted her head. Her face was red and her eyes were bright. She saw Dr. Moore, and let out a cry of delight.

"Hi, there, Dr. Moore," she said. "I never expected to see you again. How you doing?"

"I'm fine," Dr. Moore said. "But what about you? What happened?"

Mrs. Anderson laughed.

Dr. Moore asked the niece and her friends to wait,

and nodded to the orderly. She led the stretcher down the hall and into an examination booth. Mr. Anderson came stumbling loudly after them. His face was as flushed as his wife's. He flopped down on a chair and leaned loosely back. Dr. Moore sat down on a stool and looked at them. She felt she didn't know them at all. They didn't act or talk, or even look, like the Andersons she knew. She could only think they were drunk—or drugged. But she couldn't think what drugs they might have got to make them act this way. And they didn't smell of liquor.

"All right," she said. "Now tell me what happened. Have you been drinking?"

"Drinking?" Mrs. Anderson said. "Certainly not."

"We haven't been anything," Mr. Anderson said, and laughed.

"You haven't eaten anything unsual?"

"I haven't eaten hardly anything."

"Or taken any drugs?"

Mrs. Anderson let out a wail.

"Then tell me what happened."

"It was my head," Mrs. Anderson said. "You know about my headaches. Well, I got this terrible—"

"Now, wait a minute," Mr. Anderson said. "Wait just a minute. That isn't quite the way—"

"What isn't the way? I think I know—"

"But you're getting it all wrong. It wasn't—"

"Be quiet."

"Don't you tell me to be—"

"I said be quiet."

"Shut up."

"Stop it," Dr. Moore said. "Both of you. There's no reason to get so excited." She considered. They were obviously in no immediate danger. She decided to let the questioning go for a moment. They might be calmer then. And she wanted a moment to organize her own ideas. She stood up. "I'm going to leave you for a minute. Try to relax. I'll be right back."

Dr. Moore went down the hall to the house officers' corner. The resident was with a patient, but there were still two interns there. She told them about the Andersons.

"I just don't know what's going on," she said. "There's something wrong with these people. They're out of their heads. But I don't know why. The only other thing is her face is awfully red. Except that her face is always red." She stopped. "You know, I just realized something. Her husband's face is also awfully red. They've both got bright-red faces."

One of the interns cocked his head. "Like cherry red?" He said. "Like carbon-monoxide poisoning?"

"My God," Dr. Moore said. "My God—that's it."

The cause of carbon-monoxide poisoning is the inhalation of carbon-monoxide gas. Carbon-monoxide gas is generated by the incomplete combustion of some carbonaceous (wood, coal, petroleum) material. Complete combustion, however, is not a natural phenomenon. It occurs only under the most fastidiously controlled conditions. Thus, for all practical purposes, carbon monoxide is a regular product of fire. Its nature is as insidious as its generation. The presence of carbon monoxide in a room or a street or an automobile is impossible to detect by any means naturally available to man. Its anonymity is as total as that of air. Carbon monoxide is colorless, odorless, and tasteless. It even has the same specific gravity as air. It neither sinks to the ground nor rises away like smoke but mixes and mingles indistinguishably with the atmosphere.

Carbon monoxide, though always dangerous and often deadly, is a poison only in the language of convenience. It is actually an asphyxiant. It deprives its victims of the oxygen they breathe by displacing oxygen in the carrier hemoglobin of the red blood cells. This suffocating displacement is easily accomplished. Hemoglobin, by some hematological quirk, much prefers carbon monoxide to oxygen. Recent investigators have mathematically rendered its preference into odds of approximately three hundred to one. Their calculations suggest that a given concentration of carbon monoxide in the air can successfully compete for the molecular embrace of hemoglobin with anything up to three hundred times its concentration of oxygen. The result of the eager union of carbon monoxide and hemoglobin is a brilliant-red compound called carboxyhemoglobin. Carboxyhemoglobin is the source of the characteristic cherry-red flush of carbon-monoxide poisoning. It also, however, has more sinister powers. It inhibits the release of whatever oxygen has managed to combine with hemoglobin. Carboxy-hemoglobin is a stable compound, but its bonds are far from unbreakable. They readily loosen under the impact of abundant oxygen, and the hemoglobin so released, unharmed by its impetuous encounter, is free to resume its proper physiological functions. That providential frailty of carboxyhemoglobin simplifies the treatment of carbon-monoxide poisoning. It is often treatment enough to remove the victim from the poison air. A few hours of rest will then restore the normal chemistry of his blood. More seriously stricken victims can usually be rallied by the administration of pure oxygen under pressure. Unless, of course, they are already dead or dying.

It takes very little carbon monoxide to contaminate the air. The virulence of carbon monoxide is very nearly unique. A concentration of only two one-hundredths of one percent (or two hundred parts of carbon monoxide per million parts of air) can kindle in a couple of hours a dull frontal headache, and an exposure of just five minutes to air containing one per cent of carbon monoxide is almost invariably fatal. Moreover, the action of carbon monoxide is ferociously quickened by such environmental factors as heat and altitude, by the presence of debilitating disease like anemia and asthma, and by physical activity. The blood of a man at labor becomes saturated with carbon monoxide about three times faster than that of a man at rest. Mild but perceptible symptoms of illness ordinarily appear when the carboxyhemoglobin level approaches twenty per cent. More conspicuous symptoms—severe occipital headache, nausea, vomiting, dizziness, muscular incoordination, disorientation—develop as the saturation mounts toward forty per cent. At fifty per cent, unconsciousness usually descends, and a saturation of sixty-six per cent (or the conversion of two-thirds of the body's supply of hemoglobin into carboxyhemoglobin) is classically considered fatal.

The sources of carbon monoxide are abundant in the urban Western world. In the United States, they are almost everywhere. Carbon monoxide is perniciously present in the effluvia of all internal-combustion engines, most industrial plants, and many mines, mills, and workshops. There are also many domestic sources: unvented space heaters, floor furnaces, kerosene stoves, gas ranges, camp stoves, and blocked or faulty flues. Among the more familiar fuels, manufactured gas is potentially doubly dangerous, for it not only produces carbon monoxide (like natural gas and other carbonaceous materials) but actually contains it. Burning charcoal is especially rich in carbon monoxide—so rich that in France, where charcoal fires are widely used for cooking, carbon-monoxide poisoning is sometimes called *folie des cuisiniers*. Another rich source is burning tobacco. The blood of heavy cigarette smokers (those who smoke two or three packages a day) has been found to contain as much as ten per cent carboxyhemoglobin, or almost enough to cause manifest signs of illness. The most insidious source of carbon monoxide is, of course, the gasoline engine. It is also, with an ever-increasing multitude of ever more powerful automobiles on the streets, an increasingly serious one. Automobile (and motorboat) exhaust fumes contain about seven per cent carbon monoxide, and where traffic is slow and heavy the amount of carbon monoxide pumped into the air can easily approach a toxic level. A field study undertaken by the National Air Pollution Control Administration in 1967 has demonstrated that it often does. The study was conducted in ten cities (Atlanta, Baltimore, Chicago, Cincinnati, Detroit, Louisville, New York, Minneapolis, Denver, and Los Angeles) at the peak of the rush-hour traffic. Bumper-to-bumper speeds produce about three times

as much carbon monoxide as a cruising speed of forty-five miles an hour. Instruments mounted in a test car analyzed the air at the level of the driver's head. The findings ranged from a low (in Louisville) of sixty-six parts of carbon monoxide per million parts of air to a high (in Los Angeles) of one hundred and fifty-one parts of carbon monoxide per million parts of air. Concentrations of one hundred or more were recorded in four of the other cities: Cincinnati (100), Detroit (120), Minneapolis (134), and Denver (142). New York and Chicago both showed concentrations of ninety-five. The maximum allowable concentration of carbon monoxide for an exposure of several hours (established by the American Standards Association around 1900) is one hundred parts per million parts of air. Within the past few years, however, many investigators have come to believe—on the basis of certain studies on human volunteers which demonstrate that even minute concentrations of carbon monoxide can subtly dull the crucial sense of time and distance—that a concentration of one hundred is much too high for perfect safety, and they have proposed that the maximum be lowered to fifty. In the Soviet Union, the legal (though not necessarily enforced) maximum is eighteen.

It was once generally held that carbon-monoxide poisoning occurred in both acute and chronic forms. Most investigators now deny the possibility of a chronic form of carbon-monoxide intoxication. They distinguish instead between acute and chronic exposure. "Chronic exposure does not produce chronic poisoning," Dr. David H. Goldstein, professor of environmental medicine at New York University Medical

Center, noted in a 1963 medical textbook, "but, rather, repeated episodes of mild acute poisoning. Intermittent day-to-day exposures are not cumulative in effect." The incidence of severe acute carbon-monoxide poisoning has declined in the United States in recent years. This is largely attributable to the wide-spread installation of safety devices (fans, baffles, alarm meters) in industrial plants, and to safer home appliances. In New York City, for example, a total of four hundred and twenty cases of serious carbon-monoxide poisoning (a hundred and thirty-one of them fatal) was reported in 1951. The total for 1967 was seventy-three cases, of which four were fatal. Most of these cases were the consequence of dilapidated equipment, sitting in a closed car with the engine running, or a deliberate, suicidal exposure. Less conspicuously clinical cases, on the other hand, are almost certainly increasing. There are no real records of such cases, because they are seldom recognized and reported, but it is probable that thousands of Americans suffer some degree of carbon-monoxide poisoning—a late-afternoon headache, a little lurch of nausea, creeping irritability—every day. The victims are unsuspecting people who regularly expose themselves to air that, through ignorance or indifference or inadvertence, is perennially polluted. They include automobile mechanics, parking-garage attendants, traffic policemen, newspaper-kiosk keepers, cabdrivers, urban bus drivers, janitors, commuting motorists, and every now and then, a housewife like Mildred Anderson.

Dr. Moore couldn't doubt that the Andersons' trouble was carbon-monoxide poisoning. She went back

to the examination booth in a euphoria of relief. Carbon monoxide answered every question. It explained Mrs. Anderson's interminable headache, it explained the disappearance of the headache after a few hours in the unpolluted air of the hospital, it explained the return of the headache, and the dizziniess, the faintness, the weakness, the bizarre behavior. It had to be carbon monoxide, and the source could only be something in the Anderson house. Something that was regularly but intermittently in use. Something like a kitchen range, a hot-water heater, a furnace. That would also explain why Mr. Anderson had only now become sick. He hadn't been sufficiently exposed; he had only been home at night until this weekend began.

"I couldn't doubt it was carbon monoxide," Dr. Moore says, "but I couldn't, of course, just assume it. I had to be sure. I had to document it. There was a senior medical student I knew hanging around, and I grabbed him and asked him to draw some blood from the Andersons for a carboxyhemoglobin-determination test. Meanwhile, I got them both breathing pure oxygen. Then I thought of the niece. I remembered how funny she had sounded. So I rounded her up and got her on oxygen, too. Then I called the lab. The technician who could do the test I wanted wasn't on duty. I got permission to call him at home, and I called him and he moaned and groaned and carried on, but he finally got dressed and came over. A carboxyhemoglobin-determination test takes about twenty minutes, and in twenty minutes we had the confirmation: Mr. Anderson's carboxyhemoglobin level was thirty-nine percent, and Mrs. Anderson's was thirty-seven.

"By the time we got the lab reports, the Andersons were both pretty well recovered. But I kept them at the hospital. I couldn't send them back to that contaminated house. The niece threw off her little touch of poisoning very fast, and I talked to her and her friends before they left. I arranged for them to take the Andersons in until their house had been inspected. They told me the Andersons used natural gas for heating and cooking, and that the house had seemed awfully hot and a little smelly of what they now decided was gas. They said they would get in touch with the gas company the first thing in the morning. I heard the rest of the story a couple of days later. Mrs. Anderson called me. An inspector from the gas company had come out and made a thorough investigation, and my hunch had been in the right direction. The trouble was the furnace. Or, rather, the furnace flue. The inspector had found it practically blocked with fallen bricks. Mrs. Anderson thought she knew how that had happened. They had had their chimney repaired several months before—sometime back in the summer. It had needed pointing. And apparently the mason who repaired it also managed to drop a few old bricks down the flue."

[*1970*]

# A Small,
# Apprehensive Child

‑‑‑‑‑‑‑‑‑‑‑‑‑‑‑‑‑‑‑‑‑

**H**er experience was so exceptional that I'll give her an unexceptional name. I'll call her Barbara Logan. Barbara was then—in the late spring and early summer of 1968—six and a half years old. She lived with her mother, a recent divorcée, in a two-family house in the City Park section of Denver, and it was there, at around eight o'clock on the night of June 9th, a Sunday, that her experience began. It began with fever and a spasm of vomiting. She vomited off and on all night. She vomited all day Monday. She vomited all through Monday night. On Tuesday morning, she was still hot to the touch (Mrs. Logan didn't have a clinical thermometer), and she complained for the first time of pain. Her throat was sore, she said,

139

and there was a sore place under her left arm. Mrs. Logan felt and found a lump about the size of a golf ball. It was hard and painfully tender. That alarmed her. She got Barbara up and into some clothes and telephoned for a taxicab. Mrs. Logan had no regular physician. She told the driver to take them to Children's Hospital. That was the hospital nearest her home.

The driver, after a glance at Barbara, delivered them to the hospital emergency room. The physician on duty there, a woman, briefly questioned Mrs. Logan, and then turned her attention to Barbara. Her findings, which she noted on the standard chart, confirmed the cabdriver's snap impression: "Physical examination revealed an acutely ill child. Eyes sunken. Looks very miserable. Surprisingly cooperative. Lips and nailbeds cyanotic. Two-inch roughly round left axillary node, which is very tender. Mild generalized abdominal tenderness. Joints not hot or swollen. Right eardrum red. Throat slightly infected. Chest clear. Slight tachycardia [rapid pulse rate], 120. No [heart] murmur. Neck supple. Appears dehydrated. Temperature, 104.4." This last—almost six degrees of fever in so crowded a clinical context—was decisive. The physician made the necessary arrangements for Barbara's immediate admission. She also arranged for certain indicated laboratory tests (blood analysis, urinalysis, throat culture) and a chest X-ray. She did not attempt a comprehensive diagnosis. She merely noted the several apparent infections: otitis media (inflammation of the middle ear), gastritis, and pharyngitis. And added, "Rule out pneumonia."

Barbara was led up to a ward and put to bed. She

was wrapped in a cool sheet to temper her fever and given a mild analgesic for comfort. An antibiotic regimen to curb her apparent infections was begun: two hundred thousand units of penicillin every four hours, and four hundred milligrams of sulfisoxazole every eight hours. Half an hour later, she vomited. Then she seemed to feel better, and presently fell asleep. The following day, her condition was, at best, equivocal. The results of the chest X-ray were within normal limits, and any threat of penumonia appeared to be remote. Her white-blood-cell count, a standard index of infection, was only slightly elevated (to 8,300 per cubic millimeter), and the differential (or constituent) count was essentially normal. The intern assigned to the case noted on her chart, "Temperature, 100. Hydration improved. Patient extremely fussy. Nodes in axilla have increased 3-fold in nite to 15 × 10 cm. mass, which is exquisitely tender. She has had no more vomiting. Taking oral fluids. Primary culture of urine, blood & throat shows no growth. I am not impressed by her response to antibiotic therapy at this time. Will do second blood culture & watch closely."

A week went by. Barbara's condition remained uncomfortably equivocal. On Monday, June 17th, the intern noted, "Still very tender in axilla, but swelling is down. First blood culture grew Gram-negative rods at 4 days. Second culture negative at 5 days. Still has temperature 100." His second entry was a clouded clarification. A rod is a bacillus of cylindrical (or rod-shaped) conformation, and a Gram-negative rod is one that reacts negatively to a staining test developed by the turn-of-the-century Danish physician Hans Christian Joachim Gram. This reaction is a primary characteristic of numerous bacteria. Some, though only some, of these are pathogenic to man. That group, however, includes the agents of brucellosis, glanders, gonorrhea, influenza, plague, salmonellosis, shigellosis, tularemia, typhoid fever, and whooping cough. Later that day, the intern noted on the record that a sample of the cryptic Gram-negative presence in Barbara's blood had been delivered to the nearby laboratory of the Colorado State Health Department for dispatch to the Laboratory Branch of the Center for Disease Control, at Atlanta, for definitive screening and precise identification. He then returned to the bedside with a sudden discordant note: "Patient spiked temperature to 103.4." Confronted by this inscrutable turn, he reinforced the standing regimen with two new varieties of pencillin—potassium phenoxymethyl and sodium methicillin. The following day, he requested an X-ray examination of the left shoulder "to rule out possibility of osteomyelitis." The thought had apparently struck him that a fitful inflammation of the bone might be responsible for both Barbara's persistent fever and the equally stubborn swelling under her arm. If so, his mind was quickly put at rest. The roentgenologist reported on Wednesday morning that he could find no evidence of any bone involvement. Barbara's condition that morning was also reassuring. "Patient feels better," the intern noted. "Ate good breakfast. Tenderness in L. axilla diminished considerably." The sudden improvement continued, Barbara's fever fell to a scant 100 degrees. She continued to eat with appetite, and the tender swelling under her arm continued to subside. On Friday, for the first time, her temperature dropped to normal. She continued free of fever for the next four days, and on Tuesday morning, June 25th, the intern closed his record of the case. "Temperature still normal," he noted. "CBC [complete blood count] WNL [within normal limits]. Patient to be discharged today." She was discharged that afternoon, with a comprehensive supply of sulfisoxazole and supporting penicillins, to convalesce at home.

Barbara's convalescence was a fleeting one. It barely lasted over Tuesday night. She awoke on Wednesday morning with a familiar pain in her armpit. The swelling there had reappeared, and the area was now so sensitive that it hurt to even close her arm. Mrs. Logan was more confused than alarmed. Barbara, after all, had just been discharged from the hospital as recovered from whatever had ailed her. She felt Barbara's forehead. It was reassuringly cool. And Barbara said she was hungry. That surely meant there was nothing seriously wrong. She decided to wait and see. She waited until Thursday afternoon. Barbara was still cool and still able to eat with appetite, but she was also still in pain. Mrs. Logan called a cab and took her back to the hospital. "Glands in axilla have increased," the emergency room physician noted. "Now is developing enlarged nodes in left side of neck. Child does not look well. Appetite good & no fever since discharge. To return next Wednesday." Barbara did not, however, return the following Wednesday. Mrs. Logan returned her the following day. The enigmatic swellings had increased again in size and sensitivity. "Looks very poorly," the examining physician noted, and, revising his Thursday opinion, he arranged for her readmission. "Suggest surgical consultation for possible incision & drainage." Her temperature then—at eleven o'clock in the morning—was 101.4.

Barbara was assigned this time to a bed in a ward for infectious diseases. She was visited there around noon by an intern on that service. He found her to be "a small, apprehensive child with a painful, swollen left axilla" and confined his diagnosis to the merely descriptive: "Left axillary lymphadenitis." Her indifferent response to antibiotic therapy impressed him even less than it had the intern earlier in attendance. He expressed his dissatisfaction by cancelling the earlier orders. That was the usual step. The next was to mount a new and more aggressive antibiotic attack. But there he stopped, uncertain. The discarded assault was standard in what appeared to be the circumstances of the case. He reflected, and then (with the approval of the guiding resident) stepped in a different direction. Barbara, until further orders, was to be given no medication at all. The nature of those orders would depend upon the nature of the organism that had been cultured from her blood. He would wait until the report on that came through from Atlanta. It was not an easy decision, and it was not an easy wait. Barbara's condition continued as before. Her temperature returned mysteriously to normal, and the painful swellings persisted. June ended and July began. On July 2nd, the operation proposed by the admitting physician was successfully performed, and it had, as planned, the immediate salubrious effect of reducing the monstrous glands. The following day, at two o'clock in the afternoon, the report at last came through. The intern noted it on the record: "CDC called to report blood culture of 6/11/68 as suspect of *Pasteurella pestis*." That most emphatically answered his question. He could now proceed to treatment with the confidence of certainty. But it far from closed the case. *Pasteurella pestis* is the causative agent of plague.

Plague, as its prototypical name so starkly proclaims, is the oldest and most dangerous of the great epidemic diseases. The weapon with which the Lord punished the Philistines for their victory over the Israelites (and for their acquisition of the Ark of the Covenant) is generally identified as plague. Most medical historians believe that plague was probably the chief constituent of the ambiguous "Plague of Athens" described by Thucydides in his "History of the Peloponnesian War." It was plague that ravaged the Byzantine Empire in the time of Justinian (around 542 A.D.) and, according to the contemporary historian Procopius, killed half of the population. And it was plague that practically decimated Europe in the Black Death pandemic of 1348. Its appearances since then have been less dramatically lethal, but the disease is still far from conquered. Plague was more or less endemic in Europe from the fourteenth century to the end of the eighteenth century (an epidemic in Prussia in 1709 took well over three hundred thousand lives), and it continues to prevail in its classic epidemic form in much of Asia (including Vietnam) and in parts of Africa and South America. It is one of only four diseases that are still accepted by public-health authorities throughout the world as quarantinable. The other diseases whose presence aboard a ship or a plane is sufficient cause to quarantine the craft are cholera, smallpox, and yellow fever.

No disease has inspired a larger general literature than plague. Its literary fruits alone include the *Decameron* of Boccaccio, Daniel Defoe's *A Journal of the Plague Year*, and *The Plague*, by Albert Camus. The contagion from which the characters in the *Decameron* have fled to a hilltop palace near Florence is the Black Death, and Boccaccio's generally accurate description of the disease at its most relentless indicates the origin of that lurid medieval name. "In men and women alike," he notes, "there appeared at the beginning of the malady certain swellings, either on the groin or under the armpits, whereof some waxed to the bigness of a common apple, others like unto an egg, some more and some less, and these the vulgar named plague-boils. From these two parts the aforesaid death-bearing plague-boils proceeded, in brief space, to appear and come indifferently in every part of the body; wherefrom, after awhile, the fashion of the contagion began to change into black or blue blotches, which showed themselves in many first on the arms and about the thighs and after spread to every other part of the person, and in some large and sparse and in others small and thick-sown; and like as the plague-boils had been first and yet were a very certain token of coming death, even so were these for everyone to whom they came."

The black or blue blotches of the Black Death are multiple tiny hemorrhages of the skin, and occur in both of the two chief forms of plague. These forms are known as bubonic plague and pneumonic plague. Bubonic plague is the classic, and the commoner, form. It takes its name from the inflammatory swellings (so obvious to Boccaccio and so mysterious to the doctors attending Barbara Logan) of the lymphatic glands in the groin and the armpit. These traditionally definitive swellings are called buboes, from the Greek *"boubōn,"* for "groin." Pneumonic plague, as its name declares, is plague in which the lungs are involved. Essentially, it is a complication of untreated bubonic plague. Until shortly after the Second World War, when an effective antibiotic treatment for plague was found in strepto-mycin and the tetracyclines, pneumonic plague was a common consequence of bubonic plague. Untreated bubonic plague is fatal in about fifty per cent of cases. Untreated pneumonic plague is always fatal. When plague is promptly and properly treated, however, prompt recovery is the reliable rule. Bubonic plague, though easily capable of the greatest epidemic spread, often occurs sporadically. Pneumonic plague is wholly an epidemic disease, and its appearance is invariably preceded by an outbreak of bubonic plague.

Few diseases have been more portentously ex-plained than plague. Its cause was once (perhaps orig-inally) believed to be baleful conjunction of the planets Saturn, Jupiter, and Mars. It was also thought (perhaps alternatively) to be caused by other cosmic events—comets, volcanic eruptions, earthquakes. An-other, and less fortuitous, explanation attributed plague to the machinations of Jews. ("It was believed that the Jews had poisoned the wells," Guy de Chau-liac, physician to Pope Clement VI, noted in his con-temporary account of the pandemic of 1348, "and they killed them.") A more persistent view envisioned plague as one of the sterner manifestations of the Wrath of God. This attractively guilt-ridden concept (which inspired the wild-eyed peregrinations of the Flagellants in the fourteenth century) was widely embraced until almost the modern era. Even physicians accepted it, though usually with reservations. A pious seventeenth-century German physician named Johannes Raicus attempted to clarify the matter with a scholarly tract. There were, he pronounced in 1620 in his "Ex Flagello Dei," two different sources of plague. One was divine in origin and the other was a natural visitation. Divine plague, being a punishment inflicted for cause on a discovered sinner, was not infectious. The other was.

By "infectious," Raicus meant "contagious." The truly infectious, or bacterial, nature of plague was demonstrated independently by two bacteriologists, the Japanese Shibasaburo Kitasato and the Swiss Alexandre Yersin, during an epidemic of the disease in Hong Kong in 1894. A French investigator, Paul-Louis Simond, is celebrated as the discoverer of its contagious, or communicable, nature. Simond suggested, in a report to the *Annales de l'Institut Pasteur* in 1898, that the *Pasteurella pestis* of Kitasato and Yersin is not among man's natural microbial enemies. It was his correct assumption that plague is primarily a disease of rats that is accidentally conveyed to man by certain fleas. Moreover, as he proposed and as subsequent investigators were able to establish, these fleas prefer the blood of rats to that of man, and it is probable that they turn to man only when rats are scarce. An outbreak of plague in man tends to follow directly upon a decimating epidemic of plague among rats.

(The seventeenth-century French painter Nicolas Poussin precociously included among the panicking crowds in his graphic portrayal of "The Plague of the Philistines" the bodies of several dead rats.) The manner in which the flea transmits *P. pestis* to man is also accidental. A flea that has fed on an infected rat ingests a multiplicity of plague bacilli. These bacilli accumulate and eventually block the forestomach of the flea, and in order to swallow newly gathered blood it is forced to regurgitate. Much of this bacilli-laden vomitus inevitably passes into the bloodstream of the host. Plague produced by the bite of a contaminated flea is bubonic plague. Bubonic plague cannot be transmitted by ordinary contact from one human victim to another. Pneumonic plague can. Its accompanying coughs and sneezes are as irresistibly infectious as those of the common cold.

Simond's report on the role of the rat in human plague, like most such pathfinding studies, was at first dismissed as absurd. It then was acclaimed as definitive. It is now merely recalled as a milestone. For there is more to plague than Simond could suppose in 1898. More recent investigation has shown that plague is not, as he conceived, exclusively a rat-borne disease of seaport cities—the morbid consequence of the arrival in a rat-infested city of a rat-infested ship. That is only its classic approach, and one that an almost universal insistence on ratproof ship construction is rapidly rendering historic. The susceptibility of the domestic rat to plague is now known to be shared by many other wholly undomesticated rodents and rodentlike animals. Some seventy equally prolific and comparably flea-ridden creatures—including mice, rabbits, hares, voles, ground squirrels, prairie dogs, marmots, and chipmunks—are more or less hospitable to *P. pestis*. There are pockets of wild-rodent, or sylvatic, plague in the wilds of China and Southeastern Asia, in Africa, and in North and South America. One of the biggest of these enzootic reservoirs lies in the American West. In fact, it *is* the West. The area in which infected animals (and their attendant fleas) have been found embraces the states of Washington, Oregon, California, Nevada, Utah, Idaho, Montana, North Dakota, Wyoming, Arizona, New Mexico, Colorado, Kansas, Oklahoma, and Texas.

Plague is generally thought to have entered the United States with a pack of ailing rats that climbed ashore from a burning freighter on the San Francisco waterfront. Opponents of this notion suggest that plague was here long before its presence was formally noted. San Francisco, at any rate, was the scene of the first American epidemic. The epidemic began with the discovery of a dead Chinese in the rat-infested basement of the Globe Hotel in Chinatown on March 6, 1900, and it lasted, largely because the local authorities tried to hush the matter up, for almost four years—until February of 1904. It was one of the deadliest epidemics on record. One hundred and twenty-one people were stricken, and all but three of them died—a mortality rate of ninety-seven per cent. A second, and only somewhat less lethal, epidemic occurred in San Francisco in 1907, the year after the earthquake and fire. Three other American cities have experienced serious outbreaks of plague—Seattle, also in 1907; New Orleans in 1914 and again in 1919; and Los Angeles in 1924. The Los Angeles epidemic was the last recorded appearance in this country of classic, urban, rat-borne plague. It was not, however, the last appearance here of plague. Since 1908, when an epizootic in ground squirrels near Oakland, California, abruptly announced its presence, sylvatic plague has seized, along with numberless rodents, a number of human victims. One hundred and forty cases, sixty-eight of them fatal, are known. Thirty-seven (or one-fourth) of these have occurred in the past six years, and two-thirds of those recent victims have been children. Seventeen of them—like Barbara Logan—were less than ten years old.

The telephoned report on the nature of Barbara Logan's illness that Denver Children's Hospital received on the afternoon of July 3, 1968, was one of three identically alerting calls that were made that day by the Laboratory Branch of the Center for Disease Control, in Atlanta. The others went to Dr. Cecil S. Mollohan, chief of the Epidemiology Section of the Colorado State Department of Health, in Denver, and to a station of the Ecological Investigations Program of the United States Public Health Service at Fort Collins, Colorado. This last call was taken by Dr. Jack D. Poland, then acting chief (he is now the head) of the station's Zoonoses Section. A zoonosis is a disease of animals that may be conveyed to man. There are many such diseases, and the Zoonoses Section is professionally familiar with almost all of them, but the zoonosis with which Dr. Poland and his staff are principally concerned is plague. He expressed this concern in a matter of minutes with a telephone call to Denver.

Dr. Poland says, "I called Dr. Mollohan. That isn't

the way it's usually done, of course. I should have waited for him to call me. The protocol in public health is that a federal agency comes into a local matter on invitation from the local authority—the city or county or state—in charge of the investigation. But we don't stand much on ceremony with plague. I knew Dr. Mollohan would see it that way, and he did. He needed and wanted our help. I told him I'd get our people on it right away. Fort Collins is sixty miles from Denver, but that's no distance in this part of the world. Then I remembered. I said I'd do better than that. I said it so happened that Harry Hill was in Denver that day on a routine tick-fever job, and I'd round him up and send him right over. Harry Hill was Dr. Hill, a young Epidemic Intelligence Service officer assigned to us from C.D.C. I remember Dr. Mollohan laughed. That would be fine, he said, but I didn't really need to bother. Because it also so happened that Dr. Harry Hill was sitting in his office that very minute. They had been talking about tick fever when Dr. Mollohan got his call from Atlanta. So Harry Hill came to the phone, and we talked for a couple of minutes. There wasn't a whole lot to say. He knew what to do. He was a trained epidemiologist. I simply told him to go ahead and do it."

Dr. Hill says, "It wasn't quite as simple as that. There was another matter of protocol. Before I could see the patient, I had to go around to the Denver Department of Health and Hospitals and get permission. Children's Hospital is a municipal hospital. I picked up my wife—she had come down to Denver that morning with me—and I went through the necessary red tape. Then I was ready to begin. I found the intern assigned to the case, and we sat down together. He was shaken. He had just begun his training, and Barbara Logan was his first patient. There can't be many doctors whose first case turned out to be plague. He showed me her chart and gave me what he had on her personal history. Then I saw Barbara. Her clinical picture was certainly compatible with a diagnosis of plague. Anybody could have made the diagnosis—if the possibility of plague had happened to enter his mind. But it hadn't. It very seldom does. Barbara was the third case of plague in Colorado in less than a year, and both of the others were also originally misdiagnosed. One was mistaken for streptococcal sore throat and the other for tularemia. But Barbara was lucky. Or maybe she was just naturally tough. Anyway, they got her started on the right drugs in time—on streptomycin and tetracycline instead of penicillin— and she survived. She made a full recovery. The others didn't. One of them died, and the other ended up with permanent central-nervous-system damage.

"Barbara was too sick and too young for much of a talk, and I didn't stay with her long. I left the hospital and went out to the car, where my wife was waiting, and we drove back across town to the Logan house. Mrs. Logan was at home, and she was friendly and glad to help. What I hoped to get from her was some clue to the source of Barbara's infection. Sylvatic plague is hardly a common disease, but there have been enough cases over the years to establish a characteristic epidemiological pattern. The source, of course, is a wild rodent, and the setting is also wild. It's out in the wilderness somewhere, a place where wild rodents abound. For example, that fatal Colorado case I mentioned was a boy on a ranch in Elbert County who shot and carried home a prairie dog. The other case was an oil-field worker in the mountains north of Grand Junction. The incubation period in plague is from two to six days. Barbara took sick on June ninth. I naturally expected to hear from Mrs. Logan that there had been some sort of outing in the country soon after the first of June. But no. Barbara had hardly been off the block. She had been to City Park, only a few blocks away, on June fifth, and two or three weeks before that she had spent the day with an aunt on the east side of town, in Aurora, and that was all. If that was true—and how could I doubt it? —Barbara had been exposed to plague right here in the city of Denver.

"Which was crazy. Urban plague means rats. But Denver is unusual among American cities in that it has practically no rats. A continuing extermination program has just about wiped them out. However, I asked Mrs. Logan about rats. She said no. There weren't any rats, she said. There couldn't be any. An exterminator came to the house regularly. I sat and thought a minute. There had to be an animal somewhere in the picture, I said. A sick or dead or dying animal. Mrs. Logan started to shake her head, and stopped. Did I say *dead* animals? Well, she didn't know, but she had heard that some dead squirrels had been found in the neighborhood. People had been finding dead squirrels off and on all spring. That was interesting. It was even promising. Fleas will desert a host soon after its death, but plague can be contracted from infected blood or saliva. I asked if Barbara was the kind of girl who might handle a dead animal. Indeed she was, Mrs. Logan said. Very much so. She was a very inquisitive child. That was interesting, too. About these squirrels, I said—I supposed they were ground squirrels. What some people call chipmunks. Oh, no, Mrs. Logan said. They were regular squirrels. They were tree squirrels —like in the park.

"Well, I thanked Mrs. Logan and left. I didn't doubt there were tree squirrels around. The older parts of Denver are full of trees, and the Logan street was lined with big old elms. But I had always thought of plague as a disease of burrowing rodents. I went down to the car and started to get in, and saw some kids playing in the yard across the street. I told my wife I'd be right back. I went over to the kids and said I was an investigator and that I'd heard there were some dead squirrels around the neighborhood. Did they know anything about that? They all said 'Huh?' and 'What?,' and then one of them said sure—he knew where there was a dead squirrel. Did I want to see it? I said I certainly did, and he led me back around the house and out a gate and up an alley and over a fence and out another yard and across a street and around to another alley and stopped in front of a hollow tree. I looked in the hollow. I didn't have to see it—I could smell it. But there was enough of it left for laboratory examination. I went back to the car and told my wife about it and she looked sick, and we drove back to the hollow tree. There was an old fishing creel in the trunk of the car, and I scraped the remains of the squirrel or whatever it was into the creel and covered it up with an old blanket so it wouldn't smell too much. Then I looked around for a telephone and called Dr. Poland and told him what I'd found. He said O.K., bring it in. He didn't sound too excited. My wife and I had dinner and then drove back to Fort Collins. I stopped at the office and unloaded the squirrel or whatever it was and put it—creel and all—in a refrigerator in the lab, and left a note for Allan Barnes. Dr. Barnes is head of the mammalogy-entomology unit of the Zoonoses Section, and a very big man in plague. He'd take it on from there."

Dr. Barnes says, "It was a squirrel, all right—and a tree squirrel. It was the eastern fox squirrel, *Sciurus niger*. From the state of decomposition and an infestation of blowfly larvae, I judged it had been dead about a week. I handed the carcass over to Bruce Hudson in the laboratory to be tested for evidence of plague by his fluorescent-antibody staining technique. It was Dr. Hudson who adapted the F.A. test to plague. And a very good thing he did, too. The squirrel was far too dead to be tested by the standard bacteriological methods. I don't think I nourished any preconceived ideas. I felt pretty much the way Jack Poland felt. I wasn't too excited. I certainly didn't react the way I would have if Harry Hill had brought in a dead prairie dog. And I wasn't about to chase into Denver and start tearing down the Logan house looking for rats. I knew there were very few rats in Denver. I also knew that an eastern fox squirrel had been found dead of plague on the Stanford University campus back in 1966. It was an isolated case. The other campus squirrels tested out negative. But it was a case, a precedent. So I wasn't absolutely flabbergasted when Bruce Hudson walked in and told me that Harry Hill's specimen was positive for plague. It gave me a funny feeling, though. The Stanford case was a totally isolated case.

This was different. We not only had a case of plague in an urban tree squirrel. We also had a case of human plague.

"Meanwhile, of course, I'd been talking with Jack Poland and Harry Hill, and I had also been on the telephone to Denver. The people I mostly talked to there were Cecil Mollohan and Roy Cleere and Douglas McCluskie. Dr. Cleere is director of the Colorado State Department of Health, and Dr. McCluskie is director of the Division of Environmental Health for the city. The lab report was the push we needed, and we arranged for a meeting at Dr. Cleere's office on the afternoon of July eighth. That was a Monday. I went down to Denver that morning and picked up Dr. McCluskie and we drove over to the Logan house. The Logan neighborhood, I should say. We weren't looking for Mrs. Logan. We were looking for more dead squirrels. There were kids playing on the block and women going marketing and old men just sitting around, and we talked to them all. Everybody seemed to know about the squirrels. One man told us he had found a dead squirrel in his yard as far back as May. He tossed it in his garbage can. And we found three dead squirrels. A man took us to one of them, and the kids showed us the others. They looked just as dead as Harry Hill's squirrel, but they weren't too dead to test.

"That sharpened the point of the meeting with Dr. Cleere and the others. One dead squirrel was simply one dead squirrel. But four dead squirrels was a dieoff. And a die-off is always suspicious—whatever the cause of death. The other side of the picture, the human side, was fortunately unchanged. A check around the hospitals and clinics had been made, and there were no further cases of plague, or anything that even faintly looked like plague. There was still just Barbara Logan. Moreover, she would be discharged very shortly. The meeting drew up a report to inform physicians about her case and to alert them to the possibility of other victims. It reminded them of the clinical features of plague and pointed out the proper treatment. A general press release was also prepared. It gave the facts of Barbara's case, with a statement from Dr. Cleere to the effect that the situation was cause for concern but not for alarm, and it included a strong warning to the public against handling rodents, dead or alive. We also asked that any dead rodents be reported to the city health department. That about covers the meeting. Except that I was asked to head the field investigation. Dr. McCluskie and I sat down and made plans for a survey that would define the nature and extent of the infection in the animal population. Denver has a great many tree squirrels. The eastern fox squirrel was introduced in 1908. By homesick Easterners, I suppose. Anyway, it prospered. There have also been immigrants. *S. niger* used to be strictly an eastern squirrel. You never saw it west of the Mississippi. But it's been slowly moving west across the plains—living off the wheat fields and nesting in the cottonwood river bottoms—since the late nineteen-twenties. Finally, a few years ago, it joined up with the others in Denver.

"We went to work the following day. The city had the collection facilities. Dr. McCluskie mobilized his Animal Control Division, and the dogcatchers picked up carcasses wherever we had a report and turned them over to us for delivery to the laboratory for examination. Those dogcatchers really had to work. The dead-rodent reports rolled in—the phones rang all day long. Then the laboratory came through with a report on the carcasses Dr. McCluskie and I had found. They were plague-positive, too. So this wasn't anything like Stanford. This was a plague epizootic. Which brought up the crucial question of control. Control, in plague, means ectoparasite control, the eradication of the vector fleas. That was certainly all we wanted in this case. We didn't want to kill the Denver squirrels. But it was a tough nut to crack. We solved it with a system of baited stations rigged up in such a way that the squirrel got a harmless dusting of insecticide when he came onto the station. That took care of the fleas on his body, and also those back in his nest. We had some trouble with bait. Squirrels love peanut butter. But when we baited a station with peanut butter, the first squirrel to show up just settled down and ate and ate until the peanut butter was gone. We finally hit on pine cones impregnated with peanut butter. They carried those away. At the peak of our operation, we had eight hundred stations going.

"The active phase of the investigation lasted about three weeks. It began on July ninth and ran through the rest of the month. By the beginning of August, the peak of the epizootic had passed. We found our last positive on September eighteenth. And Barbara Logan was still the only human case. The total tally was eight hundred and twenty-one carcasses collected and examined. Six hundred of them were tree squirrels. The others were other animals. None of those miscellanous animals were positive for plague. Four hundred and ninety-three of the six hundred tree squirrels were found within the Denver city limits, the others on the outskirts. Only the Denver squirrels were plague-positive. The positive squirrels totalled eighty-one. The curious thing was this. We had a big block map of the city set up in Dr. McCluskie's office and we kept a record with colored pins where every squirrel carcass was found. All but six of the positive squirrels were found in the northeast quadrant of Denver—the City Park area, where Barbara lived. That would seem to be where the epizootic began and where it was somehow contained. There was also something else. The other thing was fleas. We collected a number of fleas. We found a few on newly dead squirrels, and the rest we combed off about thirty live and healthy squirrels that we trapped for that purpose. The flea to which *S. niger* is normally host is *Orchopeas howardi*, and we found the expected number of them. But we also found three other kinds of fleas. We found a species that is normally found on ground squirrels, and we found two species that are normally found on rabbits. Let me say that the only infected fleas we found—the only plague-positive fleas—were a few *Orchopeas howardi*. The wild-rodent fleas were clean. Their mere presence, however, was bad news. I'm only thankful that it happened in a city like Denver—a city with practically no rats. Because a flea transfer like that very strongly suggests a wild-rodent intrusion into the urban environment. How this intrusion may have come about I can't say. I don't know."

Neither does Dr. McCluskie. But he is willing to

guess. He says, "I think what happened was this. I think some kid caught a ground squirrel up in the mountains and brought it home, and after a couple of days he got bored with it or his parents said get rid of it, and he let it out in City Park. I think it was just an accident like that. I hope so, anyway."

[*1971*]

# The Hoofbeats
# of a Zebra

A little past five o'clock on the afternoon of October 11, 1978, a young black woman shuffled on the arm of a friend into the emergency room of Alvarado Community Hospital, in San Diego, California, and asked to be admitted for psychiatric help. Her name, she said, was Sheila Allen, her age was twenty-four, and her complaint (as later interpreted and standardized and noted on her chart) was "bizarre behavior, with looseness of thought associations and severe depression associated with suicidal thoughts." She was admitted after a brief examination to the psychiatric wing, and made comfortable there in a double room. The following day, and for several days thereafter, she was examined, tested, and variously observed. The results of these evaluations were inconclusive, and on October 16 a member of the psychiatric staff named Robert Brewer was appointed attending physician.

"I went in to see her after rounds the next morning," Dr. Brewer says. "She was sitting on the edge of the bed—sitting there with the help of a nurse. She was tall, with a beautiful figure, a beautiful face, and beautiful, wide-apart eyes. She was also pathetic. She didn't seem to have any strength at all. She couldn't walk. She could hardly sit up. She could hardly lift her arms. I introduced myself and made some getting-acquainted talk. I took her history and did a routine physical and checked her mental status. She was just as weak as she looked. She was well oriented and alert. There was some evidence of conversion hysteria. I finished up with a lot of history and a lot of problems, but no strong impressions in any direction. I was inclined to go functional, but not entirely. I did a residency in neurology, and I always try to keep the organic possibility in mind. I started thinking multiple sclerosis. Her age, for one thing, was right. Multiple sclerosis is a young-person's disease. But I'm a listener. I think that if you listen long enough your patient will usually tell you what the trouble is. So I asked her what *she* thought was her trouble. She said, 'I'm a kook.' I said maybe so, but before we go that road—I'd like you to see a neurologist I know. She almost blew up. I think she might have hit me if she'd had the strength. She said, 'I don't want to see a neurologist. I've seen a dozen neurologists. I'm a kook. I'm in the kook hospital. I want you to fix up my kookiness.' But I wasn't convinced. And that afternoon, I called Fred Baughman, the neurologist I had in mind."

I met Sheila Allen in the spring of 1983, some five years after that pitiful outburst. We met, by prearrangement, in San Diego, in the office of Dr. Brewer's neurological colleague Dr. Fred A. Baughman. She looked good—the picture of health, and beautiful, and entirely free (if she had ever been otherwise) of kookiness.

"Oh, I was," she told me. "I *was* a kook. I had to be, after what I'd been through. If a person can be driven crazy, that was me. But, of course, I wasn't really crazy. I was simply in despair. I had been sick for so long—for almost four years. I was getting sicker and sicker. I was almost helpless. I went to Alvarado Hospital because I couldn't think of anything else to do. I had finally given up.

"I don't know when my trouble actually started. I mean, it came on so innocently. I guess it began in Dallas some time in 1974. No, I'm not from Dallas. I was born in the Chicago area—in Maywood, Illinois. But when I was fourteen, my parents moved to Los Angeles, and I went to high school there. I ran track, and I was a cheerleader. I've always liked sports. I've always loved to run and dance and bike and everything like that. I went to Cal State, at Northridge, for a year, and I studied physical education. I went to Dallas because I wanted a change. There were no problems at home or anything like that. I just wanted a change. I got a job at a Sears store, demonstrating cosmetics. Then a friend told me that Braniff was hiring flight attendants. I had an interview, and they hired me and sent me to their school—six weeks of emergency procedures, first aid, posture, grammar, how to prepare the meals. I was based in Dallas, and I flew every stop to Chicago and sometimes to New York—all over. I think March of 1974 was when the trouble first began. I was out dancing one night, and my legs gave out on me. I mean, I fell down. But I was able to get right up, and I said it was my high heels. That's what I thought. So I went to lower heels, and then one night it happened again. It was just like the first time. I was able to get right up and go on. Nobody seemed to think anything of it. So I wasn't really worried. But when I had my regular Braniff physical in August, I mentioned it to the doctor. He gave me an extra careful checkup, and passed me. He said I was in great shape. He said I was probably just tired—too much standing. Well, flying is all standing. You hardly ever sit down on a flight. So that made sense. But then my legs began to hurt. I wasn't just tired, I also *hurt*—at the end of a flight, or walking through the airports. Like O'Hare. Or, especially, Dallas. You know how big it is. We were always having to walk from gate one to gate twenty-two. My legs would cramp. It was a real tight pain. I would have to sit down and rest for a couple of minutes. Then I'd be all right. But all of the girls were always complaining about being tired, so I still didn't think too much about it. Until it began to affect my arms. Just lifting two trays, and my arms would begin to tremble. It seemed like they didn't want to hold. Even a coffeepot was almost too much for my strength. I tried to get more sleep. But I just got tireder and tireder. And I began to almost miss flights because I had to sit down so often along the concourses and rest. So what I did was just get up earlier. If there's one thing I've got, it's willpower. I drove myself as hard as I could. But I was getting worried now—real worried. I went to a doctor one of my friends knew. He said take it easy. Stop driving myself so hard. He gave me a prescription for Valium.

"That would have been around the end of 1974. I thought maybe I wasn't eating right. It's hard to eat right when you're flying. All too often after we have served the passengers their lunches or dinners there wouldn't be any food left. Most of the girls carried candy bars for those emergencies. I carried what I called my survival package—tuna fish and peanut butter and crackers and raw carrots and lots of vitamins. A lot of the girls recommended a shot of bourbon at bedtime. I tried that, and it was all right, but I couldn't see that it helped me any. I had to realize that my tiredness was different from the other girls'. So finally—I think it was in October, or maybe November, of 1975—I tried again. I went to an orthopedic specialist. I told him about my legs, how weak they were—and my arms. He looked me over; he was very thorough. But he couldn't find anything wrong. He said it was probably my job—the standing and the stress and all that. His advice was to quit, to take a leave or something. But I *loved* flying. I loved my job. And I loved the money. I had a little Opel GT sports car. I had a nice apartment. I had a wonderful life. So I kept on working—getting to the airport early enough so I could make it to the gate, and getting back home late—and resting every chance I got. I stopped talking about my problems to the other girls. I didn't want them to say anything. I wanted to keep my job. But I was only fooling myself. It was just too much for me. In February of 1976, I asked for a vacation, and they gave me three weeks' leave. I went to my favorite place—to Hawaii. I relaxed and rested and tried to enjoy myself. The three weeks went by, and I was the same as always. I just didn't have any strength. I went back to Dallas and gave my two weeks' notice. I said I had personal problems. Which was true enough. My sister Enid flew in from L.A., and drove me home in my little Opel—back home to my parents.

"It's hard to explain just how I felt. I was worried about feeling so tired and weak. But I still really thought it would go away. I still really thought I'd get better. Anyway, I couldn't just sit around the house. That isn't my way. I went out and got a job—two jobs, as a matter of fact. I got a daytime job demonstrating cosmetics again. I worked in various stores doing makeup. And at night I worked as a cocktail waitress in a club. I suppose that was kind of foolish. Because I had the same old trouble—the same problem with trays, the same problem with all the standing and walking. I had to wear heels at the cocktail job, and, of course, that made things that much worse. Every now and then I dropped a tray. I could tell when it was coming on—I'd think, There goes the tray. The other waitresses dropped things, too. But they only dropped a glass or something. I dropped the whole tray. But the boss was crazy about me. That made everything OK. This was in the summer of 1976. But finally the boss got to be too much for me. I had to quit. I had already quit the cosmetics job. Two jobs were too big a load for me, and the cocktail job paid better. When I quit that, I got a daytime job as a hostess in a restaurant at the beach. I guess I knew by then that there was something really wrong, but I wanted to work. I missed the airline income. It's hard to change when you get used to a certain level of living.

"When I first came home to L.A., I had gone to the family doctor. He couldn't find anything wrong with me. Then I met a chiropractor at a party and told him my problem. He checked me out, and couldn't find anything wrong, either. He referred me to a woman psychologist. She gave me an IQ test. That only told her that I was bright. So she gave me another test. And then another. She never seemed to try to think anything out—she just kept giving me tests. I decided she was a waste of time and quit. I also quit my hostess job. I had to—I was getting weaker every day. Everything I did hurt. It hurt to comb my hair. My arms were so heavy and weak. It was hard for me to drive my car. Once or twice it was really frightening. I'd try to brake or something, and my foot wouldn't move. One Sunday afternoon I took my little three-year-old niece to the park. When we were driving home, a traffic light up ahead turned red and I started to brake and I couldn't lift my foot. Oh, my God! I thought. I'm going to kill us both. I told my niece to get down on the floor. I hung onto the wheel and we sailed across the intersection. Thank God, there was nobody coming. I don't know how I ever made it home. That was the last time I drove. I was at home now all the time. But I had problems even there. I don't know how many times my legs gave out and I fell down the stairs. They were carpeted, thank God. So I wasn't hurt much. That was going down. Climbing the stairs, I practically had to crawl. My mom was a problem, too. She kept saying I was just trying to upset her. She didn't really mean that. The real reason was that she couldn't bear to think there was something wrong with me. And my sisters. We would be getting ready to go out somewhere, and it took me so long to get ready they'd go off without me. I got so I was crying a lot. I'd try to pick up a glass, and my arm would go limp. And I'd say, 'Oh, no!'—and fall into a chair and just cry.

"But I still hadn't given up. When I quit going to that woman psychologist, my chiropractor friend suggested I see a psychiatrist. I was going out with him some, and he was really trying to help. He was convinced that my trouble was psychosomatic. I didn't know what to think. Some days I was better, and some days I was worse. Some days I could get dressed and go out and everything was almost like normal. Then the next morning I couldn't even fix breakfast. I had a drawer full of prescriptions—Valium, Elavil, Equanil, all those drugs. Every doctor I went to see prescribed something. I tried them all, and I couldn't see any difference. I couldn't see that any of them helped. So I went to a psychiatrist. He was a white guy. Some of the doctors I'd seen were white. Some were black. Anyway, I went to this psychiatrist once a week. We talked. We went over everything I'd been told by all the others. He said I must face it. I had a psychosomatic problem. I liked him; he was a nice man. He made me feel better about myself, which helped. But I didn't really believe what he said. Then I had my family—my mother and my brother and my three sisters—on me. They made it perfectly plain. They said I was crazy. I said to myself that *they* were crazy.

"About that time, in December of 1976, I met a nice guy from San Diego. He was a big guy—six foot six and two hundred and seventy pounds. His name was Ira Watley, and he had been playing offensive tackle for Miami. He'd just got cut. He was going back home to San Diego, and he suggested I come with him—get away from my family. He knew they were driving me nuts. I thought about it. Then one morning I woke up and I almost couldn't get out of bed. But I made it and started down to breakfast, and fell. I fell all the way down the stairs. I didn't know whether I was hurt or not. I hurt all over, anyway. I must have looked awful, because my mother helped me up and took me to the emergency room of a hospital a few blocks away. There was a young doctor on duty. He examined me and everything—my arms and legs and all. He said to wait, and went away. He came back with a textbook and he stood there studying it. Then he said, 'I would think you might have myasthenia gravis, but the symptoms aren't right. Myasthenia gravis starts with the eyes and face, with drooping eyelids, and trouble swallowing. You don't have that.' He said he thought I ought to see a psychiatrist. He gave me a prescription for Elavil.

"That made up my mind. I went to San Diego with Ira. He was working, so he could take care of me. He was really understanding. He wanted to get married. I didn't think so, not right then. But I was feeling a little better and getting a little restless. I wanted to do something. Ira suggested I go to school—to a business college he knew about. So I enrolled. That was in February 1977. But it was the same old story. I wasn't really any better. The school was on the second floor—a walk-up—and those stairs were too much. I would go late so people wouldn't see me struggling. It was one step and rest, another step and rest. Some days I could go three steps without resting. I was taking typing. And finally I couldn't do it. I couldn't hold out my arms. It was a three-month course, but I never finished it. After that, I just stayed home. Except to go to the doctor. I had already seen a couple of doctors in San Diego. One was a regular internist. The other was a neurologist. They were like all the rest, psychosomatic, Valium. But Ira kept pushing me to keep trying to get some help. I even went to a doctor in La Jolla who tried to hypnotize me. I wouldn't hypnotize, and that frustrated him. He told me I didn't want to get well. Then I tried an orthopedic surgeon. He asked me to lift my arms. I couldn't do it. He stomped out of the room. He said he couldn't help me because I wouldn't cooperate. Then I tried another psychiatrist. I had four or five visits. The psychiatrists and the psychologists were all alike. What did your last doctor say? I see. Well, I agree. Psychosomatic. I'm going to give you a prescription for an antidepressant. Some of them started with my childhood. Some started now and worked back. I told them I had a normal childhood—a normal middle-class childhood. I told them I didn't hate my parents, and they didn't hate me. They were loving parents. The psychiatrist I went to four or five times, he saw Ira when Ira brought me to his office. I told you Ira is a very big man. So this doctor had a new idea. He asked me if Ira beat me.

"I started getting completely worse in June—June of 1978. Ira was away. The Winnipeg Blue Bombers had signed him on, and he was training up there in Canada. He had arranged everything before he left. He had his father come over and look after me. He sent me his check every week, and one of his friends— Frank or Drake—would take me to the bank and to the supermarket or wherever. Frank was very sympathetic. He had been in Vietnam and had had a hard time there, and he'd had some therapy. He persuaded me to try the state mental-health center. I joined their group-therapy class. I went for a while. But the classes were kindergarten stuff, and I wouldn't take the drugs they offered. Elavil was one of them, and it actually seemed to trigger more weakness. It seemed to actually loosen my muscles. I had some bad experiences even without drugs. I'd sit down in a chair, and when I wanted to get up I couldn't. I'd have to wait for Ira's dad or somebody to help me. It got so I was afraid to cook. I remember one afternoon I had some vegetables on the stove. I left the kitchen and fell, and I couldn't get up. I just lay there smelling them burn. The house was full of smoke when Ira's dad came in and turned off the stove. It was an awful feeling. I wasn't good for anything. I used to sit and meditate and pray. I'd fix my mind on, say, fishing or shopping, and try not to think of anything else. I did a lot of praying. I'd say the Lord's Prayer over and over and over. It helped me, I think. I prayed in bed in the morning, too. I kept a Bible by the bed. In the morning, when I woke up, I'd read or pray, and finally I'd have the strength to get up. One morning, I couldn't comb my hair. I didn't have the strength. I finally had to lay my head on the sink, and that way I could use my arms a little. There was another time. Drake and his brother Lee took me fishing with them out on the park dock. After a while I went to the bathroom. I sat down on the toilet, and I couldn't get back up. Nobody came in. I yelled and yelled, and finally Lee came in and got me out.

"I think that was about the last time I went out anywhere. I knew I was reaching the end of the line. My muscles were getting weaker and weaker. I had to rest more and more. I knew that pretty soon I'd be helpless. I had to do something before it was too late. I decided my only hope was to get hospitalized. And I knew the best way I could get hospitalized was to talk depression and suicide. That was one thing I'd learned from all those psychologists and psychiatrists. The hospital I picked was Alvarado Community Hospital. It was the nearest one to Ira's apartment. I got Frank to drive me there, and he had to practically carry me into the emergency room. I told my story, and they took me in. I remember the date. I remember it very well. It was Wednesday, October 11, 1978, late in the afternoon. But the date I really remember is the following Wednesday, October eighteenth, around noon. That was the day I met Dr. Baughman. He came into my room and looked me over and told me what my trouble was. I had myasthenia gravis."

"Well, yes," Dr. Baughman told me. "It *was* almost as quick and easy as that. I was pretty sure the minute I saw her that her trouble was myasthenia gravis. The only other possibility was amyotrophic lateral sclerosis, and she was much too young for that." Dr. Baughman is a slight, wiry man of fifty, with a bang of sandy gray hair and a wide, warm, country-boy smile. He was smiling now. "But it wasn't magic. Myasthenia gravis is a special interest of mine. I trained at Mount Sinai, in New York, and Mount Sinai has a rather famous myasthenia gravis research laboratory. Some important work has been done there. So I learned about myasthenia gravis early, and it is always on my mind. There is a saying about diagnosis—about why doctors often fail to recognize one of the less-common diseases. It goes: When you hear hoofbeats, you don't necessarily think of a zebra. I recognized the hoofbeats of a zebra. That was my only magic. I won't say myasthenia gravis is a common disease. But it isn't a rarity, either. The national occurrence rate is one in twenty thousand. I see my share—because I'm a neurologist and because I'm aware. I average three to five *new* cases a year. Women seem to be more susceptible than men—particularly young women. Myasthenia gravis is a good descriptive name. The 'my' refers to muscle, and 'asthenia' comes from the Greek for weakness. It isn't as gravis—as serious—a disease as it once was. It was first described in the seventeenth century, and it was named around the end of the nineteenth century, and in those days and up until the middle 1950s it was very often fatal. There is a treatment now. But, of course, it can't be treated if it isn't diagnosed. That's the problem. In that respect, Sheila was a classic case.

"I remember my first look at Sheila. Bob Brewer had called me and said he had some doubts about a psychiatric patient at Alvarado and would I take a look. So the next day I went up to Four South when I finished my regular rounds. The first order of business is the visual impression. And oh, Lord! She was pathetic—truly pathetic. She was lying in bed and not exactly crying—sort of whimpering. There was a feeling of just hopelessness. Her beauty made it all the worse. I knew the moment I saw her that there was a profound generalized muscle weakness. I called a nurse, and we got her sitting up. She tried to help, but it was a genuine, real weakness. Nothing functional about it. Her face was normal, and so was her speech. There was a slight nasal character, but not much. I had the nurse get her to her feet and walk. It was a definitely abnormal gait; it was a waddle. That indicated a hip-girdle weakness. We have a scale of evaluation. It begins at zero, then trace, then poor, then fair, then good. Sheila's hip and shoulder girdles were poor to fair. Her body and feet were in the good range. The weakness was symmetrical, and there was just no question about it. I knew her history, and I didn't believe a word of all those psychiatric evaluations. This was a serious muscle disease.

"It's sad to think how close she came to an early diagnosis. I'm thinking of that young doctor up in Los Angeles. He suspected myasthenia gravis, but he made the common mistake of going entirely by the book. The books all emphasize that the presenting symptoms are drooping eyelids, facial weakness, and palatal weakness—difficulty in speaking. The classic teaching requires the presence of one or more of those symptoms for a diagnosis of myasthenia. I had one patient who was referred to me by an ophthalmologist. A man had come to him complaining that he was losing his eyesight. The ophthalmologist recognized that the cause of his failing sight was the drooping eyelids of myasthenia gravis. I wish the textbooks

were a little less rigid. But the fact is that a mere suspicion of myasthenia is enough, because there's a
quick and easy diagnostic test that is almost entirely
reliable.

"Myasthenia gravis is a fundamentally mysterious
disease. I mean the basic cause is unknown. It is generally thought to be one of the several autoimmune
diseases—the consequence of some disturbance in
the body's immune system. Antibodies appear in the
blood that interfere with the supply of a substance
called acetylcholine, which mediates neuromuscular
function. I'm putting a highly complicated process in
very simple terms. The result of this inhibition is a
weakness much like the weakness induced by the poison curare, and the treatment of myasthenia gravis
has derived from an understanding of curare intoxication. The site of the physiological defect in both
curare poisoning and myasthenia gravis is the neuromuscular junction. In the absence of acetylcholine,
the muscular response very rapidly decreases. A period of rest will, at least for a time, restore sufficient
acetylcholine to allow for normal function, but only
for a limited time. Then the weakness returns. Drugs
have been developed that are antagonistic, in varying
degrees, to the substance that inhibits acetylcholine.
One of these anticholinesterase agents is involved in
the diagnostic test for myasthenia gravis. Tensilon—
or, generically, edrophonium chloride—has the power
to restore almost normal muscular function almost instantly, in a matter of moments. Its effect lasts only
moments, but a positive response to Tensilon is diagnostic of myasthenia gravis.

"Tensilon was developed at Mount Sinai in 1952,

and I've used it many times. The effect is always startling. I gave Sheila the usual dose—ten milligrams, injected intravenously. I waited a moment, and then checked her arm strength. There was resistance to pressure—maybe eighty to eighty-five percent of normal. So I asked her to get up and walk. She said, 'You know I can't walk.' I told her to try. She gave me a doubtful look—and sat up. Then she stood up. Then she walked across the room. It was a miracle. It's always a miracle, but this was one of the most miraculous. I'll never forget the look on her face. She was dazed. She was stunned. The tears were running down her cheeks. I felt the way I always do when I see that miracle happen. I felt—I don't know—almost godlike. Then she began to give out. I helped her back to bed. She collapsed. It was all over."

Sheila Allen was discharged from Alvarado Community Hospital on the morning of Thursday, October 26, 1978. That was fifteen days after the day of her admittance and eight days after her dramatic noonday meeting with Dr. Baughman. In the course of those eight days, she was introduced to another, and more durable, anticholinesterase agent called Mestinon, and an effective dosage (one sixty-milligram tablet every four hours) was determined. Tensilon is of only diagnostic value. The discharge summary noted: "Discharged to out-patient treatment, to be followed by Dr. Patricia Marrow for supportive psychotherapy (in adjusting to the presence of a chronic debilitating illness) and by Dr. Fred Baughman for control of myasthenia gravis." Her condition, the summary added, was "markedly improved." It was, indeed. The friend who had helped her into the hospital was there to meet her on her departure. She was pleased by his thoughtfulness, she was glad to have his company, but she didn't need his help. She walked out of the hospital with the easy gait of any normal twenty-four-year-old woman. She was, for all practical purposes, a normal young woman, and two weeks later, in early November, she was leading a normal life. She had a job demonstrating cosmetics at a San Diego department store, and she was attending evening classes at a school for real-estate brokers.

Dr. Baughman saw Miss Allen at his office soon after her hospital discharge, and once a month thereafter. At their December meeting, on December 5, he noted that her response to Mestinon was entirely satisfactory. It was better than that of many other patients in his experience, and inferior to none. Nevertheless, he watched her closely and questioned her closely at their monthly meetings. There is always a chance that Mestinon, or any other anticholinesterase agent, may in time weaken in its mastery. There is a surgical procedure that can provide a vigorous supplement to Mestinon therapy. This involves the removal of the thymus gland. The thymus is situated between the chest wall and the windpipe, just below the thyroid gland. Its function has to do with the development and maintenance of the immunological system. The thymus develops rapidly in infancy, grows more slowly until around puberty, and then, in most people, begins to wither away. It has been established that in victims of myasthenia gravis the thymus is abnormally intact, and its functions seem to have been perverted into the phenomenon of autoimmunity. Dr.

Baughman decided in the course of the summer of 1979 that Miss Allen would benefit from the removal of her thymus, and he arranged with a thoracic surgeon named David M. Long to perform the operation. Miss Allen was admitted to El Cajon Valley Hospital on September 25, and underwent a transcervical thymectomy the following morning. The operation was a complete success, and its good results were immediately apparent. Dr. Baughman noted that within less than two hours Miss Allen's muscular powers were stronger than at any time since he had diagnosed her illness. She was discharged, stronger than at any time in recent years, on September 29.

"Oh, sure," Miss Allen told me toward the end of our talk in Dr. Baughman's office. "I knew that a thymectomy was a serious operation. Dr. Baughman told me all about it. But, of course, I agreed. Whatever he suggested was gospel to me. He was the messiah. He *is* the messiah. I moved back to Los Angeles in January of 1980, but we keep in touch—I'm still on Mestinon; I always will be—and I see him here once a year. It seems to me that I feel better every day. When I moved back to L.A. I had finished my real-estate course, and I went in with my mother and father in their real-estate business. I also did volunteer work for a while in a hospital in the neighborhood. I did physical counseling. Then in 1982 I heard about a new airline opening up with flights between L.A. and Hawaii, and I applied, and they took me on. I'm a senior flight attendant, and I do seven turnabout flights a month. Between trips, I still work in real estate. The only trouble I have now is trying to hold myself back. I don't want to walk—I want to run. I'm *so* full of strength and energy. I guess I'm making up for lost time. I told my new boyfriend about my myasthenia. He said, 'So what?' We dance all night."

[*1984*]

# Index

184